ZACHARIAS TANEE FOMUM

THE WAY OF CHRISTIAN CHARACTER

ÉDITIONS DU LIVRE CHRÉTIEN
4, rue du Révérend Père Cloarec
92400 Courbevoie France
editionlivrechretien@gmail.com

Published by

EDITIONS DU LIVRE CHRÉTIEN

4, rue du Révérend Père Cloarec

92400 Courbevoie - FRANCE

Tél : (33) 9 52 29 27 72

Email : editionlivrechretien@gmail.com

Table des matières

Préface 7
Christian character 9
Love 34
Joy 48
Peace 59
Patience and long-suffering (endurance) 76
Generosity and gratitude 91
Humility, meekness, and lowliness 107
Discipline (self-control) 126
Mercy and kindness 159

Very important 171
About the author 175

Préface

This book, *"THE WAY OF CHRISTIAN CHARACTER"* is the fifth in the Christian Way Series. The titles of the books in this series are:

- Book 01: The Way of Life
- Book 02: The Way of Obedience
- Book 03: The Way of Discipleship
- Book 04: The Way of Sanctification
- Book 05: **The Way of Christian Character**
- Book 06: The Way of Spiritual Power
- Book 07: The Way of Christian Service
- Book 08: The Way of Spiritual Warfare
- Book 09: The Way of Persecution
- Book 10: The Way of Prayer
- Book 11: The Way of the Overcomers
- Book 12: The Way of Encouragement
- Book 13: The Way of Loving the Lord
- Book 14: The Way of

Christian character is all-important. The Lord Jesus wants all His disciples to be like Him in their character. He has put the Holy Spirit in each believer to work that character out.

Only those whose character conforms in every way to that of the Lord Jesus can be said to be truly entirely sanctified.

This book is about the character of Christ in the life of the Christian. We send it out with prayer that the Almighty Father should use it to work out the character of His begotten Son in His adopted sons.

Zacharias Tanee Fomum,

B.P. 6090, Yaounde - CAMEROON.

Christian character

The Lord is deeply concerned about character. It is His primary purpose that those who know Him should be like Him in the content of their character. It is in this sense that we are told of the first apostles that, *"He appointed twelve, to be with him, and to be sent out to preach and have authority to cast out demons"* (Mark 3: 14-15). They were appointed first to be with Him so that, in being with Him, they might become like Him in character and, only secondarily, to be sent out to preach and cast out demons. It can be rightly said that only those who have been with Him and, therefore, put Him on, can be sent out by Him to minister in His name. All who have not been with Him and have, therefore, not put on His character, are excluded from serving Him. The first call of the Lord is that people may come to Him and be changed to be like Him. Ministry is a secondary issue. It is in this wise that the apostle Paul wrote, *"My little children, with whom I am again in travail until Christ be formed in you!"* (Galatians 4:19).

Christ formed in the believer = Christian Character.

If a person's life does not resemble that of the Lord Jesus, his service for Him will not mean much. There are many who talk about the Lord today and even attempt to serve Him, but their character speaks against what their lips proclaim. It was said of one preacher that he was as evangelistic as an angel but twice as wicked as the devil. This is most tragic.

There is the gospel that is preached by the lips, but there is another gospel that is preached by character - by life. It is the purpose of GOD that the two "gospels" should become the one Gospel - a presentation of the Lord of glory. Without this gospel preached by word and life, we shall have a hard time in convincing a watching world of the reality of Christ. The world is tired of spoken Christianity that is not backed by life. The truth is that the lives of many believers speak very loudly against the Gospel. Many have looked into the lives of many believers to see discipline, love, tenderness, firmness, etc, which are characteristics of Christ, but have failed to see these traits.

There has been an emphasis on the gifts of the Holy Spirit today in the Churches and even in the world and, to some extent, this is but right, seeing that His gifts were laid aside for too many years. However, let us be aware that gifts are not graces. Balaam continued to prophesy even on the way of disobedience. Samson continued to manifest unusual physical power while manifesting unusual moral powerlessness. Spiritual gifts do not necessarily mean that the person exercising the gifts is spiritual or holy. The Lord warned us when He said, *"On that day many will say to me, 'Lord, Lord, did we not prophesy in your name, and cast out demons in your name, and do many mighty works in your name?' And then I will declare to them, 'I never knew you; depart from me, you evildoers'"* (Matthew 7:22-23).

It is obvious that Christian character is more important than spiritual gifts. However, no one should understand us as saying that spiritual gifts are not to be greatly desired. They have their place in the life and ministry of the believer and the Church, but for sustained ministry before God, both now and in the future, it is character - life, that counts more.

It is sad that it seems quite acceptable in Christian circles that a believer should be undisciplined, self-willed, proud, touchy, dirty, talkative and critical, and yet not be considered sinful, provided he does not commit fornication in action, steal, murder physically, etc. So we have a whole list of sins (the character traits of the devil) that believers commit with a "good" conscience, while claiming to be holy and filled with the Holy Spirit and while maintaining a spirit of high censorship on other believers who are equally as sinful, except that their sins fall into the class of "forbidden" sins.

This message is a heart's cry that all of us who name the name of the Lord should depart not only from the "deeds of darkness," but also from those sins that seem to be acceptable to others but which the Lord hates. May no believer rest until he has fully and wholly put on the character of Christ.

I do not write as one who is already perfect, yet l believe that l have seen the problem and found the answer in the Lord Jesus and, like Paul of old, l am pressing on relentlessly for the mark of the upward call of God in Christ Jesus. To this purpose - pressing on to maturity in Christ - I invite all who love the Lord Jesus.

1. MARKS OF THE CHARACTER OF THE DEVIL

(THE CHARACTER OF THE UNBELIEVER AT ITS WORST. THIS IS ACQUIRED BY DESTROYING ALL THAT WAS RECEIVED FROM THE CREATOR AND THE GOOD TRAITS RECEIVED FROM ANCESTRY)

Lack of sweetness. Lack of tenderness. Manifestations of a bitter and frustrated personality.

1. An unforgiving spirit
2. Impatience
3. Irritability
4. Being easily upset
5. Anger
6. Wrath
7. Harshness
8. Bitterness
9. Callousness (no deep feelings for suffering people. Pitilessness)
10. Hardness of heart
11. Rejoicing at evil
12. Jealousy
13. Worry
14. Inconsiderateness
15. Mercilessness
16. Unkindness
17. Being easily offended
18. Sowing discord
19. Revengefulness
20. Rudeness
21. Exposing the faults of others.

Insecurity and Self-centredness. Extreme extroversion or introversion.

1. Self-pity
2. Indifference
3. Selfishness
4. Withdrawn personality
5. Uninvolvedness
6. Passive attitude
7. Lovelessness
8. Joylessness
9. Self-induced misery
10. Unfriendliness at a deep level
11. Inferiority complex
12. Negative attitude (a capacity to see all as going wrong)
13. Coldness
14. Weakness.

1. Pride
2. Arrogance
3. Conceit
4. Haughtiness
5. Spitefulness
6. Fastidiousness (being difficult to please)
7. Self-sufficiency
8. Stubbornness
9. Ingratitude
10. Self-advertisement
11. Love of praise
12. Superiority complex
13. Slyness
14. Jealousy
15. Being difficult to approach

16. Being distant
17. Hardly accepting faults
18. Being difficult to correct
19. Self-justification
20. Prejudice
21. Narrow-mindedness
22. Disrespectfulness
23. Waiting for others to approach one
24. Hiding personal faults
25. Pretentiousness
26. A critical spirit
27. Often feeling ill at ease.

Indiscipline and lack of self-control.

1. Indiscipline
2. Unfaithfulness
3. Instability
4. Being easily moved and easily changeable
5. Impulsiveness (acting on the spur of the moment)
6. Superficiality (lacking deep thought)
7. Talkativeness
8. Laziness
9. Rashness
10. Cowardice
11. Foolishness
12. Fearfulness
13. Indulgence
14. Extravagance
15. Lying

16. Deliberately presenting false impressions of self or others
17. Untidiness
18. Being disorganized
19. Dirtiness
20. Being easily discouraged
21. Uncontrolled speech
22. Divulging of secrets.

2. NATURAL CHARACTER (HOW ACQUIRED)

1.   At natural birth.

At natural birth, the one born receives character traits from God as Creator and from his ancestry. The traits received from God as Creator are all good and those received from ancestry are a mixture of good and bad. Somehow each child bears some traits that come from the type of ancestors that the child had. These are not learnt. They are just there. For example, it has been clearly shown that children behave like their parents in some ways, even if these parents died on the day the child was born.

2.   Received natural character in the crucible of life.

What is received from God as Creator and what is received from ancestry constitute the basic elements of the person's natural character. As the child grows, the traits received at birth will develop. The direction of their development will depend upon the circumstances of life that the person experiences, from the moment of birth, as the person grows up, and how that person reacts in each circumstance. So, received natural character will be modified by:

1. Circumstances
2. People
3. Things that one encounters along life's way.

Take, for example, someone may live in a greedy, competitive society. This will influence him to some extent in the direction of greed and competition. He may face criticisms and failure that create self-doubt and withdrawal into self. He may feel ignored so much so that he has to advertise himself, etc. He may live with thoughtful people and that may help him to be thoughtful. He may be taught to be grateful and so he will acquire that trait, and so it goes.

Depending on the circumstance, people and things that come a person's way and the way he reacts to them, his final adult character may be pleasing or distasteful. Each person's natural character is then the product of what he received and the choices he made. These things can be summed up as follows:

At natural birth. Traits of character received from God as Creator and from ancestry.

Fully developed natural character being the sum of what has remained of that which was inherited and that which was destroyed or built in response to the circumstances of life, people and things.

Each situation presents a person with a choice, for example:

1. The choice to smile or to frown.
2. The choice to be warm or cold.
3. The choice to be tender or hard.
4. The choice to exalt or to press down.
5. The choice to force oneself out or to force oneself in.
6. The choice to greet or to wait to be greeted.
7. The choice to rejoice or to be sad or to be indifferent.

At each point of choice there is the way of least resistance and the more difficult way. Character is built by human choices and confirmed by whether the person chooses the way of least resistance or the more difficult way. Each person is, to a large extent, the product of his choices.

3.   The dangers of natural character

Let me, first of all, say that the world is a far better place to live in because of the many unbelievers in it with many traits of character that are received from God as Creator. For example, there are tender, kind, generous, humble, etc, unbelievers. They received these traits from the Creator and have allowed them to blossom with time.

God in Christ summed up all that was in the old creation (received from God as Creator) and sentenced it to death on the cross in one decisive act. In so doing, God revealed His evaluation of all that is of the old creation, all that is natural.

God's verdict on the old creation with its good and bad elements is, "Away with it." God has decided that all that is of the old creation cannot serve Him along with what is received from Him at the beginning of the New Life.

Because God has only one place for the old creation (the cross), all the elements of character that are received from Him as Creator and not as Father in the Lord Jesus, must be gotten rid off.

It is alright for an unbeliever to function in God's world by using natural character traits. However, when the unbeliever becomes a believer, he is called upon to reject these traits, abandon them to the cross and, then, through resurrection, put on Christ.

Good natural character traits that have been through death and then resurrection can be used by the believer to serve the Lord.

The reason why a believer cannot use his natural abilities to serve God and satisfy the Lord is that such a person is of necessity unstable. Take natural love for example. A person with such a love will love all those who please him. The number of people in such a person's circle may be large, yet he will love them. However, when faced with an enemy, what will happen to this capacity to love? It will betray itself. It will fail. Unbelievers cannot love their enemies. God's twice born children can. The Lord Jesus said, *"You have heard that it was said, 'You shall love your neighbour and hate your enemy.' But I say to you, love your enemies and pray for those who persecute you, so that you may be sons of your Father who is in heaven; for he makes his sun rise on the evil and on the good, and sends rain on the just and on the unjust. For if you love those who love you, what reward have you? Do not even the tax collectors do the same?"* (Matthew 5 43-46).

Take another example of a person who is naturally joyful. Everything will go well until he is stricken with great sorrow and then it will be found that, because his joy was rooted in nature, it could not stand in circumstances that needed the supernatural joy of the Lord. Take another person who is naturally generous. He will continue to give and give for as long as his gifts are accepted and gratitude expressed. But what if they are unappreciated? Something will crack in him and die! However, the person in whose life the Holy Spirit, by way of the cross, has worked out giving, will give and give, irrespective of how his gift is treated. He will give like God who gave His only Son to undeserving sinners and who gave His Holy Spirit to those who murdered His only Son.

When a person has believed in the Lord Jesus, he must co-operate with the Lord Jesus to ensure that his natural endowments are yielded to death on the cross and then to resurrection. Resurrected natural endowments are the talents with which believers can serve God. All other talents are not only useless in divine service; they stand on God's way. For example, a naturally tender person is more likely to disobey God when called upon to rebuke someone than if he did not have that natural attribute.

3. MARKS OF THE CHARACTER OF THE LORD JESUS (THE CHARACTER OF THE CHRISTIAN AT FULL MATURITY)

Marks of sweetness and tenderness. A capacity to feel with people at a deep level.

1. A forgiving nature
2. Patience
3. Long-suffering
4. Tenderness
5. Sweetness
6. Rejoicing at good
7. Goodness
8. A quiet spirit
9. Calmness
10. Peacefulness
11. Compassion
12. Graciousness
13. A capacity to feel deeply with people
14. A pitiful heart
15. Endurance
16. Mercifulness
17. Considerateness
18. Kindness
19. Being difficult to offend
20. Sowing unity
21. Politeness
22. Covering the faults of others.

Secure and self-giving. Humble.

23. Assured (confident)
24. Involved
25. Generous
26. Exuberant
27. Committed
28. Single-minded
29. Loving
30. Joyful
31. Friendly
32. Glad
33. Caring
34. Strong
35. Concerned
36. Warm

1. Humble
2. Meek
3. Self-effacing
4. Tolerant
5. Possessing a capacity to accept help with gladness of heart
6. Grateful
7. Easy to get along with
8. Lowly of heart
9. Confident
10. Having a positive attitude (a capacity to see that the best can come)
11. Straightforward
12. Easy to approach
13. Accepting faults easily
14. Easy to correct

15. Open-minded
16. Broad-minded
17. Respectful
18. Approaching others
19. Exposing personal faults
20. Unpretending
21. At ease always
22. Relaxed.

Disciplined and well-controlled personality.

1. Disciplined
2. Hardworking
3. Faithful
4. Trustworthy
5. Thoughtful
6. Reflective
7. Deep (thinking profoundly)
8. Taking initiative
9. Stable
10. Firm (capable of exerting discipline)
11. Truthful
12. Having insight
13. Courageous
14. Wise
15. Bold
16. Tidy
17. Organized
18. Clean
19. Persistent
20. Having controlled speech
21. Keeping secrets.

4. CHRISTIAN CHARACTER (HOW ACQUIRED)

1.   At Natural Birth:

Traits received from God as Creator and from ancestry.

Treatment by circumstances of life: The influence of:-

1.   Circumstances
2.   People
3.   Things.

Natural Character (the character of an unbeliever)

2.   At New Birth: The crisis of conversion.

A young believer indwelt by the Holy Spirit has natural character plus special impartations received from God as Father in Jesus Christ. Some traits come on suddenly by special acts of God, so that some aspects of the person change completely. Some negative attributes of natural character disappear at once.

C.

3.   Two Ways for Further Development of Character

A	B
The cross for the breaking down of all that remains of natural character. Natural character gives way as it is progressively dealt with by the Cross. The Cross uses:-	The Holy Spirit for building up into full likeness of Christ, i.e, the putting on of Christ.
	The fruit of the Spirit is all present in miniature form.
4. The circumstances of life, e.g, Humiliation for the proud: You think you are wonderful and someone comes and tells you the reverse, or you are allowed to fail repeatedly, etc.	The fruit of the Spirit grows as it is nourished by:-
5. Co-operation with the Holy Spirit in putting off all that is of nature by saying, "No, no, no," to the desires of the flesh.	7. Loving the Lord 8. Studying the Word 9. Obeying the Lord 10. Serving the Lord 11. Fasting 12. Suffering joyfully

6. Suffering which results in natural confidence being taken off. 4) Discipline: Refusal to do or say things which you would naturally have loved to do or say. And refusal to go to places to which you would naturally have loved to go. You commit yourself to do the right things which you would naturally not love to do. You become God's prisoner.	13. Discipline: Doing things that on your own you would not want to do, like:-
	   n. Talking well of your enemies.
	   o. Doing good to those who oppose you.
	   p. Continuing to work when you are tired.
	   q. Etc.
	18. Submission to the will of God with gladness.

MATURE CHRISTIAN CHARACTER : Christian character (how acquired)

Christian character has a sevenfold origin:

1. The purification through death and resurrection of all that was received naturally from God as Creator.

2. The purification through death and resurrection of all that is good that was received from ancestry.

3. That which is specially imparted by the Lord to the person at the moment of conversion.

4. That which is specially imparted to the believer by the Lord along the years of the Christian pilgrimage.

5. That which comes as a further development of (1), (2), (3) and (4) in the School of Suffering and along all of life's way.

6. That which comes by the destruction, and getting rid of, by the cross, of all that is bad and was received from ancestry.

7. That which comes by the destruction, and getting rid of, by the cross, of all that is bad (unchristlike) which was learnt along life's way.

The first five points will enable a person to put on the character of Christ that is summarized in the table, and the last two points will enable one to get rid of the marks of the character of the devil that have also been summarized in an earlier table. The putting on and the putting off are necessary for the full character of Christ to be expressed.

The Bible says, *"If then you have been raised with Christ, <u>seek</u> the things that are above, where Christ is, seated at the right hand of God. <u>Set your minds</u> on things that are <u>above</u>, not on things that are* *on earth. For you have died, and your life is hid with Christ in God. When Christ who is our life appears, then you also will appear with him in glory"* (Colossians 3:1-4).

"*Put to death therefore what is earthly in you: fornication, impurity, passion, evil desire, and covetousness, which is idolatry. On account of these, the wrath of God is coming upon the sons of disobedience. In these you once walked, when you lived in them. But now put them all away: anger, wrath, malice, slander, and foul talk from your mouth. Do not lie one to another, seeing that you have put off the old nature with its practices and have put on the new nature, which is being renewed in the knowledge after the image of its creator*"(Colossians 3:5-10).

The Bible continues to say, "*Put on then, as God's chosen ones, holy and beloved, compassion, kindness, lowliness, meekness, and patience, forbearing one another and, if one has a complaint against another, forgiving each other; as the Lord has forgiven you, so you also must forgive. And above all these put on love, which binds everything together in perfect harmony. And let the peace of Christ rule in your hearts, to which indeed you were called in the one body. And be thankful. Let the word of Christ dwell in you richly, teach and admonish one another in all wisdom, and sing psalms and hymns and spiritual songs with thankfulness in your hearts to God. And whatever you do, in word or deed, do everything in the name of the Lord Jesus, giving thanks to God the Father through him*" (Colossians 3:12-17).

So it is obvious that Christian character will not just come from nowhere. It will become the lot of those who actively co-operate with the Holy Spirit. In this, there are a number of things that are indispensable. These include:

1. Seeking the things that are above. Seeking Christlikeness in character.

2. Setting the mind on the things that are above.

3. Setting the mind away from the things that are on earth.

4. Putting to death what is earthly (unchristlike character marks).

5. Putting away all the unchristlike character marks that have been put to death.

6. Putting away the old nature with its practices.

7. Putting on the new nature with its practices.

8. Putting on love.

9. Allowing (letting) the peace of Christ to rule in the heart.

10. Allowing (letting) the Word of Christ to dwell richly in the person.

We can then say that Christian character is acquired by two basic steps:

1. Having the right vision: The mind set on Christ and spiritual things and away from the world and worldly things. This is very important because people will ultimately become what they have set their minds to become. You will accomplish your goals as far as your character is concerned. If you set your mind to become like Christ, you will accomplish it. Be careful about the things you like, for you will have them.

2. Putting off all that is unchristlike. This will not happen on its own. Make a list of the character traits of the Enemy that you find in your character. Do not spare yourself. Do not deceive yourself that you are what you are not. You may find very many things on that list that are in your life. Face up to them and tell God, "I am this bad." Again I say, do not cover them up. Do not give yourself false consolation by saying that others have their weaknesses too and that you are not alone. This will not help. Do

not blame someone else for your character faults. Own them up. Ask God to enable you to put these negative characteristics to death and to put them away. Be serious about this. If you are serious with God, He will do two things for you:

a. He will take away some of the undesirable characteristics at once, all of a sudden in answer to your prayer.

b. He will hand you over to the dealings of the cross. If, for example, you are proud, He will arrange you to face circumstances where your pride will be hurt. For example, if you think you are very attractive, you will face circumstances where your attractiveness will be totally useless or someone will come your way and, to your shock, will tell you that you are ugly. If you see yourself and repent, God will begin to take your pride away, but if you just find ways of excusing yourself and blaming the one who said that you were ugly, God will arrange other circumstances to bring you down. If you have been boasting about your ability and intelligence, He will allow you to fail an examination so that you are humble. If you continue to boast, He will allow you to fail again and again and allow other people whom you thought were so inferior to you to do better than you. He will not spare you until you have learnt the lesson and then submitted to Him from the heart, confessing that you are nothing.

1. Putting on all that is Christlike. Again as before, this will not happen on its own. It will take place in the lives of those who mean business with God and who are determined that the character of Christ in all its fullness will be manifested in their lives. So, if you look at the character traits of the Lord Jesus and face up to the lack

of many of them in your life, you may want to bow down before God and say to Him that you are not what you ought to be and that He should make you into what you should be. If you are sincere, God will do two things for you:

b. He will impart some of the characteristics of Christ to you in great measure in one supernatural act so that you can suddenly, with the touch of God, become grateful whereas before you were not, or He can give you a generous spirit which you did not have before, all at once.

c. He will take you through suffering, testings, trials, etc, until that which is lacking is put there by Him or, that which was undeveloped is allowed to develop. It is said of the Lord Jesus: *"For it was fitting that he, for whom and by whom all things exist, in bringing many sons to glory, should make the pioneer of their salvation perfect through suffering"* (Hebrews 2:10).

The Lord Jesus was perfected through suffering. The disciples must be perfected, like Him, through suffering. The more a person suffers for the Lord, the more like Christ he becomes. The more he is squeezed, pressed, frustrated, opposed, contradicted, etc, and he receives all without grumbling, the higher he climbs up the ladder of Christ-likeness. The Bible says *"More than that, we rejoice in our sufferings, knowing that suffering produces endurance, and endurance produces character..."* (Romans 5: 3,4).

1. The fruit of the spirit

The fruit of the Spirit is really the total character of Christ. Every believer at the moment of the new birth possesses the potential for all the aspects of the fruit of the Spirit to be manifested in his life, but only those who co-operate with the Holy Spirit see the fruit mature and mature quickly in them. There are no fruits of the Spirit. There is just the fruit of the Spirit. This is humbling; for no one can afford to boast until the whole range of the fruit has come to ripen in his life.

1. The conflict

The Lord Jesus is anxious that His children bear His character in every respect. The wicked one is also anxious that all who are his own and, in addition, the twice-born children of the Kingdom of God betray their Lord by being like him (the devil) in character. There is, therefore, conflict. The Bible says, *"For the desires of the flesh are against the Spirit, and the desires of the Spirit are against the flesh; for these are opposed to each other, to prevent you from doing what you would"* (Galatians 5:17). *"But the fruit of the Spirit is love, joy, peace, patience, kindness, goodness, faithfulness, gentleness, self-control; against such there is no law. And those who belong to Christ Jesus have crucified the flesh with its passions and desires"* (Galatians 5: 22-24).

The child of God must actively decide to take sides with the Lord in this conflict and thus mature in Christian character.

1. God will win

The Bible says, *"Christ loved the church and gave himself up for her, that he might sanctify her, having cleansed her by the washing of water with the word, that he might present the church to himself in splendour, without spot or wrinkle or any such thing, that she might be holy and without blemish"* (Ephesians 5: 25-27).

We know that:

1. Without spot talks of sinlessness.
2. Without wrinkle talks of the first love and zeal that has not cooled through the years of waiting.

3. Holiness talks of separation and consecration.

4. Without blemish talks of character faultlessness.

Because the Lord will have a Church that is in splendour, He will bring all who are truly His to sinlessness, wrinklelessness, blemishlessness and in holiness. So we are sure that all true believers will be brought to perfection in character. God will win. God must win. The question is, "How soon?"

1. First-fruits

We know that the Lord Jesus will first come to take those who are ready in the rapture. Those believers who co-operate the fullest with the Holy Spirit will be brought soonest into the perfection of God and qualify to be raptured as the first-fruits. Those who do not so co-operate, who are complacent or sympathetic with their character faults, will be left behind to go through and be perfected in the great tribulation.

You have a choice now with regard to your character as to whether you will be part of the choicest first-fruits unto God or not. This is a most serious matter and you had better settle it at once.

1. Be patient with God

As we have already said, God will bring all who are His to perfection. He is out to do that, and nothing will deter Him. All believers are called to be patient with Him as He works things out in them. What He needs in His children is their full co-operation in working things out. The rest is His Work.

Many of God's children will discover on close examination that their character is truly distorted. They may never have truly faced themselves before and, on coming face to face with what indeed they are like, they may be shocked; for the things they considered wonderful in the past are now seen for what indeed they are - distortions. Four possibilities are open to the child of God at such a point:

1. He may feel very discouraged and say that it will be impossible for his twisted personality to be put right. This discouragement is from the Enemy and all who yield to it remain in bondage.

2. He may take it lightly and say that he has been like that all his life and there is nothing that can be done about it. Such ease will only lead to permanent damage, for God has no sympathy for those who are at ease in Zion.

3. He may worry and fret over his character so much so that he cannot do anything for God. He may possibly say, "I will wait to be perfect in character before I can serve God." Such a one will also fail, for worry is a sin and God cannot help him to be like Christ while he is given over to worrying. The Bible says, *"And which one of you by being anxious can add one cubit to his span of life?"* (Matthew 6: 27). We, too, ask, "And which one of you by being anxious can add an iota of Christlikeness to his character?"

4. He may take his character analysis to the Lord and say to Him, "Lord, I am not what You want me to be. I am distorted. I want You to change me. I cannot change myself. I am prepared to submit to the discipline of the cross so that Your character may be worked out in me. I will obey You and wait on You to do it. I surrender to You now and ask You to work as soon as possible and with the greatest degree of depth, to ensure that I am what You want me to be."

Those who make the fourth possibility theirs will find that God takes them seriously and begins the work of their character transformation slowly or quickly as the need may be. Sometimes it will be so painful that the one under transformation may feel like giving up, but nevertheless, he must press on with the Lord. He must refuse to justify himself when he fails. He must regard all lack of tenderness as sin, all acts of indiscipline as sin, all disorderliness as sin, etc. He must confess such sins and insist that God should make him different, and God will do it.

There are two main stages in which God works to make anyone like Christ in character. First comes either a major crisis followed by the gradual process of what God wants to do (moulding, refining, purifying, etc), or the gradual process that prepares him for the crisis. Take, for example, someone who is very proud about his intelligence. The crisis will come when suddenly he fails a major examination and the results are known in the circles where he is used to exalting himself. To a self-confident woman it might come as she suddenly wakes up to the fact that she has lost the warmth and affection of her husband because she is dirty and he hates dirt. These are major events and then there are the other small ones that come along daily as the cross destroys that which must be destroyed and the Holy Spirit in turn builds in its place that which is of the Lord. The one who will make a success of it in the shortest possible time will not despair, but say with the apostle, "*And we all, with unveiled face, beholding the glory of the Lord, are being changed into his likeness from one degree of glory to another; for this comes from the Lord who is the Spirit*" (2 Corinthians 3:18).

Glory be to the Lord!

Love

Love is the most important facet of the fruit of the Spirit. We must put on love first, then put on the other aspects of the fruit and seal it all up with love. Without love, spiritual gifts, spiritual power and Christian discipleship are meaningless. The apostle Paul writes, *"If I speak in the tongues of men and of angels, but have not love, I am a noisy gong or a clanging cymbal. And if I have prophetic powers, and understand all mysteries and all knowledge, and if I have all faith, so as to remove mountains, but have not love, I am nothing. If I give away all I have, and if I deliver my body to be burned, but have not love, I gain nothing"* (1 Corinthians 13 1-3).

To put all this in mathematical terms we can write:

1. The spiritual gift of tongues love = Spiritual zero.
2. Prophetic and spiritual knowledge

    capacities love = Spiritual zero.
3. All faith love = Spiritual zero.
4. Total sacrifice love = Spiritual zero.
5. Martyrdom love = Spiritual zero.

So a person can accomplish some of the greatest feats in the spiritual realm and yet score spiritual zero in the realm of love, and pass before God for a complete failure. No wonder the apostle says, *"Make love your aim"* (1 Corinthians 14:1).

We can put love into three categories. There is a third-class kind of love. This is the "if" type of love. This kind of love says, "If you do this and that, l will love you," or "If you are this and that, l will love you." The object of love has to work very hard to deserve the love. Only a few people can qualify for this kind of love. There is a second-class kind of love. This is the "because of" kind of love. This kind of love says, "Because you are kind, loving, gentle, etc, l love you." The person is loved for what he is. It is based on some merit which, if lost, will result in the cessation of the love. It is a higher kind than the "if" type, but all the same the permanence of the love is not guaranteed. The person may sooner or later cease to be loved. For example, if someone is loved because he is kind and handsome, a day may come when he becomes unkind or is involved in an accident that destroys his handsome looks, and thus he could lose what caused him to be loved.

There is a first-class kind of love. This kind of love is the "in spite of" type. This first-class kind of love says, "You may have all these faults and lack this and that, but l love you." This is a self-disinterested love for others that gives itself away to those who deserve and to those who do not deserve love. It is the kind of love that flows out irrespective of what the object of love is or does. It is the type of love that the Lord Jesus manifests and which all believers are called to manifest.

f.   God is love

God loves in a total sense. He is love. He is total love. He is perfect love. The Bible says that God is love (1 John 4:

7,9,16). God is not only love but God loves. The Bible says, *"For God so loved the world"* (John 3: 16); *"God so loved us"* (1 John 4: 11). God's love was purposeful. All true love has a purpose in view. True love has a goal that has nothing to do with just the passing interests of the person loved. All true love has heavenly motives. The goal of love is that we may live (1John 4:9). He loved us and sent Jesus Christ for us, so that we might not perish but have eternal life (John 3:16). These are the "positive" acts of His love. "Negatively," His love blocked the way to hell by raising the cross of His Son as a permanent barrier. Many people think of love merely in terms of feelings. Love is feelings plus something more than feelings. God did not just stay in heaven and have a warm feeling of love towards lost sinners. The warm love that He had led to far-reaching action. Love is manifested in deep actions.

g.   God's love was manifested to the undeserving

The Bible says, *"But God shows his love for us in that while we were yet sinners, Christ died for us"* (Romans 5:8). God has nothing personal to gain from loving us. He has always been self-sufficient. We were the ones who benefited 100% from His love. He gained nothing while we gained everything. He gave everything. We had nothing and we received everything. It was not because God saw something good in us that He loved us. It was not because He saw some future profit which He could make out of us. From the cross to the Kingdom, God has been and will always be on the giving end and man on the receiving end. Glory be His holy Name!

h.   God's love accepted no obstacles

Our sins were enough to put Him off, but He refused to be put off. Where our sin abounded in indescribable abundance, His love, grace, mercy and self-giving over-abounded. The Bible says, *"Law came in, to increase the trespass; but where sin increased, grace abounded all the more"* (Romans 5:20). True love refuses to be put off.

1. CHRISTIAN LOVE

a.   Origin and quantity

Christian love is the love of God imparted to the believer through the Holy Spirit. The Bible says, *"God's love has been poured into our hearts through the Holy Spirit which has been given to us"* (Romans 5:5).

The love of God has not been given to the believer in small quantities. It has been poured out into the believer. The measure that is in the believer is dependent on how much there is in God, and we know that there is absolutely no limit to love in God, since His whole being is love.

Every believer has all the love in himself that he needs to satisfy God and all in the body of Christ. God has indeed given without measure. No believer should pray and say, "Lord, give me more love for this person. Lord, give me some love for this other person." These are escapist prayers. They shift the responsibility to love away from the believer where actually it is.

If there is limitless love in each child of God, then why is it that the Church is love-starved? Why are there so many in the Church who need love and do not receive it? The answer is simple. Far too many believers do not want to give love. They do not want to let that which God has poured out into them flow out unto others. Believers are either selfish and hoard the love or they do not allow it to flow, because of self-love. Self-love manifests itself in the fear to love under the pretext: "I may be rejected. I may be ignored. l may get hurt." The fear to get hurt is a true manifestation of self-love, and true love and self-love are mutually exclusive.

That the reason for not loving is not the absence of love but the refusal to love is seen in the most loveless believer. When he has chosen the one he wants to love, there is no limit to what will be poured out and showered on that one. For the others, a tourniquet is applied so that nothing flows out, but to the preferred one, the tourniquet is removed in full. To others, it is removed in part. By a constant process of applying in full or applying in part or a total removal of the tourniquet, that person's love pattern is set up. The tourniquet can also be used to block oneself from receiving love. We insist that all believers have from the Lord, an unusual reservoir of love. Whether they actually love or not is dependent on their wills and the pattern of release or withholding of love which they build for themselves over the years.

b.   Characteristics of Christian love

The Bible says, *"Love is patient and kind; love is not jealous or boastful; it is not arrogant or rude. Love does not insist on its own way; it is not irritable or resentful; it does not rejoice at wrong, but rejoices in the right. Love bears all things, believes all things, hopes all things, endures all things. Love never ends"* (1 Corinthians 13: 4-8).

We can isolate eight positive characteristics of love.

Love:

1. is patient
2. is kind
3. rejoices in the right
4. bears all things
5. believes all things
6. hopes all things
7. endures all things and
8. is eternal (never ends).

Where there is love there is patience, and who can love and fail to be kind to the object of love? Who can love and not rejoice with the good of the beloved? Who will not bear with the one he loves? Who would dare to distrust the one he loves? Who does not hope the best for the one he loves? Who does not endure trials that come to him because of the one he loves? Who would give up the one he loves?

We can isolate eight characteristics that love does not have.

Love:

1. is not jealous
2. is not boastful
3. is not arrogant
4. is not rude
5. is not irritable

6. is not resentful

7. does not insist on its own way

8. does not rejoice at wrong.

We can say: Jesus is patient and kind, rejoices in the right, bears all things, believes all things, hopes all things, endures all things, never ends. We further say: Jesus is not jealous, boastful, arrogant, or rude. He does not insist on His own way; He is not irritable, or resentful, and does not rejoice at wrong. If we replace Jesus by your name, will it sound true or untrue?

Many believers, instead of loving, hate. They hate actively or passively. To ignore a person, to treat him as if he did not exist, is to hate him. To see a person's need and refuse to do something to meet it is to hate the person. Also, to refuse to find out a person's need is to hate him. We can isolate the following characteristics of hatred.

Hatred:

1. is impatient

2. is unkind

3. rejoices at wrong

4. bears nothing

5. believes nothing

6. hopes nothing

7. endures nothing

8. ends in death.

Hatred:

1. is jealous

2. is boastful

3. is arrogant

4. is rude

5. insists upon its own way

6. is irritable

7. is resentful.

We can clearly say that the devil is impatient, unkind, rejoices at wrong, bears nothing, believes nothing, hopes nothing, and endures nothing. The devil is jealous, boastful, arrogant, rude, irritable, resentful. He ever insists upon his own way, and always rejoices at wrong.

If we replace the devil with your name, will it sound as an accurate or as an inaccurate description of you? This should make you think. You should substitute your name in place of the devil and weigh things carefully in your heart, then maybe you need to fall on your knees and beg God for mercy.

2. THE COMMANDMENTS TO LOVE

1.   The old commandment

God gave man the old commandment of love which said, *"You shall love your neighbour as yourself"* (Leviticus 19:18). This commandment applies to all the people in the world. Believers are to love their neighbours as themselves; yet how many can say they do? How many of us even know who our neighbours are? How many of us have identified their need and are doing something about it? Do we not instead talk lightly of their misery, sin and plight? This is tragic. It calls for deep repentance and for restitution by loving. If our neighbours are in practical need and we do not reach out to their need, we disqualify ourselves from being witnesses to them.

2. The new commandment

In addition to the old commandment meant for all of mankind, there was a special commandment from the Lord Jesus to His disciples. He said to them, *"A new commandment l give to you, that you love one another, even as l have loved you, that you also love one another. By this all men will know that you are my disciples, if you love one another"* (John 13:35).

We are to love the people of the world as we love ourselves, but love the brethren the way Christ loved us. How did Christ love us? He gave Himself away for us. He laid His life for us. He said, *"This is my commandment, that you love one another as l have loved you. Greater love has no man than this, that a man lay down his life for his friends. You are my friends if you do what l command you"* (John 15:12-14). *"By this we know love, that he laid down his life for us; and we ought to lay down our lives for the brethren"* (1 John 3:16). The new commandment demands that l manifest my love for all the brethren and for each one of them individually by laying down my life for them. These are the demands of love.

Love demands that l give myself away completely without holding back anything, not even my life.

The Lord did not leave this kind of love as an option to the Church. He left it as a command. It must be obeyed. Failure to obey to love is sin, just like theft, immorality, etc.

3. FAILURE TO LOVE

If a believer does not love, what will that mean? It will mean the following:

1. He does not know God (1John 4:8).
2. God does not abide in him (1 John 4:12,16).
3. He does not love God (1 John 4:20).
4. He does not keep God's commandment (1 John 3:23).
5. He is in darkness and walks in darkness (1 John 2:9-10).
6. He is a murderer (1 John 3:15).
7. He abides in death, *"We know that we have passed out of death into life because we love the brethren. He who does not love abides in death"* (1 John 3:14).

Brethren, this is most serious. What the Bible is saying is that if there is one brother or one sister, just one, whom you do not love, you are abiding in death. l want to ask you a personal question, "Are you abiding in death?"

4. LOVING OUR ENEMIES

There will be people (believers and unbelievers) who hate us; who are our enemies. Are we then exempted from loving them? Does their attitude towards us exempt us from fulfilling the Lord's command to love them? No! Certainly not. We are not to make enemies. We are to love everyone. If anyone decides to make himself our enemy, we must leave that to him and love him on our own part. People may have us for their enemies, but we should love them.

The Lord Jesus said, *"Love your enemies and pray for those who persecute you, so that you may be sons of your Father who is in heaven; for he makes his sun to rise on the evil and on the good, and sends rain on the just and the unjust. For if you love those who love you, what reward have you? Do not even the tax collectors do the same? And if you salute only your brethren, what more are you doing than others? Do not even the Gentiles do the same? You, therefore, must be perfect, as your heavenly Father is perfect"* (Matthew 5: 44-48).

Loving is not just a feeling. It is the taking of a realistic attitude to the needs of others. You may not feel a special warmth in your heart for your enemy, but you must act to meet his need. This is love. The Bible says, *"If your enemy is hungry, give him bread to eat; and if he is thirsty, give him water to drink"* (Proverbs 25:21).

5. THE PRACTICE OF LOVE

The emotions of the believer need to be released for the love that God has poured in our hearts by the Holy Spirit to fully manifest itself. Ask the Lord to release your emotions, so that you can flow out to people. Actively decide that you are going to let yourself flow out to others. Look out in particular for someone who needs love and give yourself in love to that person. Love gives. Take a gift to the person.

Identify someone who hates, dislikes or ignores you and love him. Find out what his need is. Meet his need. Give him a gift. Do not run away from him. Seek his company and be a blessing to him. He may speak evil of you, speak well of him. Trust the Lord to change his attitude towards you.

As you flow out to others, you create more room for the Lord to flow into your being and increase your reservoir of love. Those who love increase their love capacity. Those who give themselves away in love find that they do have more of themselves to give away and they also possess a huge capacity to receive love.

Those who hold themselves back and refuse to flow in love <u>shrivel</u> and die inwardly. The one who wants to be loved more must love more, and the one who is to receive much love must give much love away. The law of sowing and reaping is quite applicable here. *"The point is this: He who sows sparingly will also reap sparingly, and he who sows bountifully will also reap bountifully"* (2 Corinthians 9:6). *"Give, and it will be given to you; good measure, pressed down, shaken together, running over, will be put into your lap. For the measure you give will be the measure you get back"*(Luke 6:38).

6. LOVING SPECIAL PEOPLE

The Bible nowhere demands that we should love everybody equally. We are to love everyone, but we can love some more. Everyone should receive the minimum of our self-sacrificing love, but others can have more.

The Lord Jesus loved all the disciples and loved them to the end. However, He was very close to Peter and James, and John. John was the beloved disciple. The Lord also loved Martha, but Mary was especially close to Him.

If you love someone or some people in the Church in a special way, you have only to ensure that your relationship does not exclude others, that it is a blessing to the whole body and that it satisfies the heart of God.

7. LOVE - ETERNAL

The Bible says, *"Love never ends"* (1 Corinthians 13:8). Prophecies will pass away. Tongues will cease and knowledge will pass away. Brethren, let us grow in love; for it is the thing that will not pass away. We are encouraged to make love our aim (1 Corinthians 14:1). Yes, let us make love our aim. We must not just allow things to take their natural courses. We must humbly come before the Lord and make the love that flows from Him our way of life.

In addition to making love our aim, we must grow in love. We must make progress. The apostle exhorts believers in the following way, *"And it is my prayer that your love may abound more and more, with knowledge and all discernment"* (Philippians 1:9). *"And may the Lord make you increase and abound in love to one another and to all men, as we do to you, so that he may establish your hearts unblameable in holiness, before our God and Father, at the coming of our Lord Jesus with all his saints"* (1 Thessalonians 3: 12-13).

8. LOVE - THE FINAL MOTIVE

Only that which is done out of love for God and man will stand the test of fire on that day. All else is self-seeking. The Bible says, *"Let all that you do be done in love"* (1 Corinthians

16:14). Let all that you do be done out of love. This is the way of the Lord. Amen.

Joy

A joyful person rejoices. Joy and rejoicing are invariably linked. Joy is the contentment of the heart; the outflow of a life filled and possessed by God.

1. THE ORIGIN OF JOY

God the Father, the Son and the Holy Spirit is the origin of all true joy. All who want joy must go to this Source. The Psalmist says, *"There are many who say, 'Oh that we might see some good! Lift up the light of thine countenance upon us, O Lord!' Thou hast put more joy in my heart than they have when their grain and wine abound"* (Psalm 4:6-7). So God the Father is the Source of joy.

"These things l have spoken to you, that my joy may be in you and that your joy may be full" (John 15:11); *"But now I am coming to thee; and these things I speak in the world, that they may have my joy fulfilled in themselves"* (John 15:13). The Son, the Lord Jesus, is the Source of joy.

"For the kingdom of God is not food and drink but righteousness and peace and joy in the Holy Spirit" (Romans 14:17). The Holy Spirit is the Source of joy.

Because God is the Source of true joy, all who truly possess joy rejoice in Him. The Psalmist said, *"Then I will go to the altar of God, to God my exceeding joy"* (Psalm 43:4).

2. REJOICING IN THE LORD

Rejoicing is the outflow of joy. When joy is full it overflows in rejoicing. There are many things that can give us some joy, but those whose joy is permanent are those who have found God as their one Source of joy. They rejoice in Him and are satisfied in Him. They do not look elsewhere to passing things. Because God is unchanging, unaltering, and unmovable, their joy is permanent. Their joy, being rooted in the Lord, is not governed by outward circumstances. We are called to rejoice in the Lord.

Psalm 33:1-3:

"Rejoice in the Lord, O you righteous! Praise befits the upright. Praise the Lord with lyre, and make melody to him with the harp of ten strings! Sing to him a new song, play skilfully on the strings, with loud shouts."

Isaiah 61:10:

"I will greatly rejoice in the Lord, my soul shall exult in my God; for he has clothed me with the garments of salvation, he has covered me with the robe of righteousness."

Joel 2:23:

"Be glad, O sons of Zion, and rejoice in the Lord, your God; for he has given the early rain for your vindication, he has poured down for you abundant rain, the early and the latter rain, as before."

Habakkuk 3:17-18:

"Though the fig tree do not blossom, nor fruit be on the vines, the produce of the olive fail and the fields yield no food, the flock be cut off from the fold and there be no herd in the stalls, yet I will rejoice in the Lord, I will joy in the God of my salvation."

Luke 1: 46-47:

"My soul magnifies the Lord, and my spirit rejoices in God my Saviour."

3. WHO ARE THOSE WHO REJOICE?

8. *Those who seek the lord rejoice:*

"O give thanks to the Lord, call on his name, make known his deeds among the peoples! Sing to him, sing praises to him, tell of his wonderful works! Glory in his holy name; let the hearts of those who seek the Lord rejoice" (1 Chronicles 16:8-10).

9. *Those who take refuge in the lord rejoice*

"But let all who take refuge in thee rejoice, let them ever sing for joy; and do thou defend them, that those who love thy name may exult in thee" (Psalm 5:11).

10. *The righteous rejoice*

"Rejoice in the Lord, O you righteous!" (Psalm 33:1). If you are one of those who seek the Lord or one who takes refuge in Him; if you are righteous, then rejoice in the Lord.

4. THE REJOICING OF THE WORLD

The people of the world do rejoice, but their joy is not from the Lord. Therefore, it soon passes away. It is like the joy of players whose team has scored a goal in a football match. They are excited. They jump and they embrace each other and the whole world is seemingly under their feet. Soon the opposite side scores and their joy evaporates completely. The joy of the world, born out of material and passing situations, never lasts. We do not make that our aim.

5. THE REJOICING OF GOD'S CHILDREN

It is the will of God that His children should always rejoice. Theirs is to be a permanent joy, not dependent on man or things, but on God Himself. The Word of God commands us as follows:

Philippians 4:4 *"Rejoice in the Lord always; again 1 will say, Rejoice."*

1 Thessalonians 5:16 *"Rejoice always..."*

The believer is commanded to rejoice always. He is to rejoice at all times, in all circumstances. Not to obey this command is to sin. Miserable Christians are not obeying this command.

Such rejoicing will not come naturally. We shall have to co-operate with the Holy Spirit to have it. I dare say that God has done everything that is necessary for us to have permanent joy. He has given Himself and given us all that we need in Christ Jesus. He has put His joy in us. The Lord Jesus considers the disciples as already possessing the joy that comes from Him.

He does not admonish the disciples to look for joy. Rather, He asks them to ensure that no one takes away their joy (John 16:20-22).

So the Lord expects that when outward circumstances are unfavorable, we shall still rejoice. He says, *"Blessed are you when men revile you and persecute you and utter all kinds of evil against you falsely on my account. Rejoice and be glad, for your reward is great in heaven, for so men persecuted the prophets who were before you"* (Matthew 5:11-12). *"Blessed are you when men hate you, and when they exclude you and revile you, and cast out your name as evil, on account of the Son of man! Rejoice in that day, and leap for joy, for behold, your reward is great in heaven; for so their fathers did to the prophets"* (Luke 6:22-23).

6. FULL JOY

All God's children possess some amount of joy. However, the Lord wants our joy to be full and overflowing. John the Baptist always rejoiced in the Lord, but there was a day when his joy was complete, full. On that day, he saw that eyes were now turned from him and turned on Jesus. He saw all people going to Jesus (John 3:26). Then he said something very far-reaching. He said, *"He who has the bride is the bridegroom; the friend of the bridegroom, who stands and hears him, rejoices greatly at the bridegroom's voice; THEREFORE THIS JOY OF MINE IS NOW FULL. He must increase, but 1 must decrease"* (John 3:29-30). Jesus said, *"Ask, and you will receive, that your joy may be full"* (John 16:24). John said, *"And we are writing this that our joy may be complete"* (1 John 1:4).

7. How can a person attain unto full joy?

We have already said that all believers have joy. The question is how this joy can be perfected and brought to the fullest. From John the Baptist, we learn a number of lessons about the secret of full joy.

First of all, he surrendered all his own interests. He was not interested in spiritual greatness. He was not interested in a following. Had these been his interests, he would have known only sorrow as the Lord Jesus increased in popularity. He was interested only in the Lord Jesus and in the greatness of the Lord. If your sole ambition is the greatness of Christ, you will know full joy.

Secondly, John was humble. He considered himself unworthy to loosen the thong of Jesus' sandal. He was anxious to decrease, that Christ might increase. He said that he was only a voice crying that the way of the Lord be prepared. The proud of heart can know nothing of full joy. They will know temporary joy, but God and the circumstances of life will always fight against them to deflate them. So they will be unsteady in their rejoicing.

To be joyful, a person must come to the point where he is satisfied in the Lord and in the Lord only. The Psalmist said, *"He only is my rock and my salvation, my fortress; I shall not be greatly moved" (Psalm 62:2). "For God alone my soul waits in silence"* (Psalm 62:1). How can such a one know disappointment?

The Bible says, *"Cast all your anxieties on him, for he cares about you"* (1 Peter 5:7). Things may be going wrong. Cast all of them on Him. You will then have no burdens, and your heart will be free to rejoice and rejoice to the fullest.

If you know where your reward is, you will rejoice exceedingly. Those who know that their reward is in heaven, and seek no rewards here, will maintain perfect joy. Take, for example, some brethren who make a gift to someone and the person is not grateful. They become very upset and lose their joy. They wanted some reward here and their joy was tied to it. Since the reward was not forth-coming, they were miserable. Are you seeking a heavenly reward or an earthly reward? If your reward is heavenly, then, even in the midst of persecution, you will rejoice.

Another way to maintain complete joy is to avoid the company of miserable people. Children from miserable homes are miserable. How is your closest friend? Is he joyful or miserable? You will become like him. Also, ask and receive from the Lord. The Lord said, "Ask, and you will receive, that your joy may be full."

We can sum up this whole matter of how to be joyful in this way:

J - Jesus: Putting Jesus first in all things, at all times and in all places.

O - Others: Putting others next in all things, at all times and in all places.

Y - Yourself: Putting yourself last in all things, at all times and in all places.

The person who puts Jesus first, others next and himself last will without doubt, radiate with the joy of the Lord. Make that your aim.

8. THE MANIFESTATION OF JOY

Some believers are always looking miserable, but they want to deceive us that they are full of joy. Joy, when it overflows, comes out to the surface. Of course, all true joy, being a fruit of the Spirit, is inward in origin, but it does not remain inward. It flows outward.

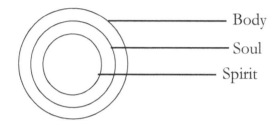

If your joy is small, it will remain in your spirit.

If it is greater, it will get to your soul.

If it is allowed to increase, it will reach your body.

When fully released, it will flow through you to others.

If your joy cannot be seen on your face, it is not full. I know some brethren who have become less joyful with increasing years in the Lord. They tell me it is because they are becoming more spiritual. All who are truly spiritual will overflow with joy. I am not saying that they are not praying more, giving more to the Lord, or serving Him more. They are. But as long as their joy is no longer being seen, it is sure that they have missed something of the special touch they had with Him at the beginning. Serving Him has replaced Him in their hearts.

Full joy will be manifest. It is always like a child's: heartful, expressive and overflowing. Joy has an emotional part.

Some think that frowning is spiritual and laughter carnal. Well, God laughs. The Bible says, *"He who sits in the heavens laughs"* (Psalm 2:4).

Joy is sometimes manifested in excitement. The Bible says, *"And when he has found it, he lays it on his shoulders, rejoicing. And when he comes home, he calls together his friends and his neighbours, saying to them, 'Rejoice with me, for I have found my sheep which was lost'"* (Luke 15:5-6). What do you think this man looked like while he carried his lost but now found sheep back home? I am sure of one thing. He was wearing no long face. He was all smiles and excitement. He could not contain himself. That was an expression of joy. Let us express our joy that way.

When one sinner repents, we are told that there is joy in heaven. I do not believe that angels are without emotions. They rejoice. They shout and praise the Lord. Have you ever done that or are you religious, sanctimonious and sad?

We are told to leap for joy during the time of persecution, since we know the reward that awaits us. Leaping and shouting are an expression of joy.

Joy is also and often manifested in song. The Bible says:

Psalm 47:1

"Clap your hands, all peoples! Shout to God with loud songs of joy!" Have you ever clapped your hands and praised the Lord with loud shouts of joy? Begin today.

Psalm 43:4

"Then I will go to the altar of God, to God my exceeding joy; and I will praise thee with the lyre, O God, my God."

Psalm 92:4

"For thou, O Lord, hast made me glad by thy work; at the works of thy hands I sing for joy."

Psalm 98:8

"Let the floods clap their hands; let the hills sing for joy together."

Singing! Songs that flow spontaneously without effort, without self-consciousness are the lot of Spirit-filled people. I know that when people are filled with the Holy Spirit, they rejoice and their joy comes forth in song.

9. THE BELIEVER: A SOURCE OF JOY TO OTHER BELIEVERS

The apostle said to Philemon, *"I have derived much joy and comfort from your love, my brother, because the hearts of the saints have been refreshed through you"* (Philemon 7). May God help us to walk with Him and be a source of blessing to the Church so that many may derive joy and comfort from us. I ask myself, "Am I a source of joy to others?" I ask you, "Are you a source of joy to others?" When they see you or hear of you, do they rejoice?

10. THE BELIEVER : A SOURCE OF JOY TO GOD

The Bible says, *"For as a young man marries a virgin, so shall your sons marry you, and as the bridegroom rejoices over the bride, so shall your God rejoice over you"* (Isaiah 62:5).

The Lord is looking for His special lovers over whom He may rejoice. May you and l become such, and we shall be truly blessed. Glory be to His holy Name!

Peace

Peace is the absence of war, conflict or noise. It is tranquility, quiet of soul and rest.

1. THE AUTHOR AND SOURCE OF PEACE

God the Father is the Eternal Peace. He is also the Eternal Source of Peace. The Bible says, *"Now may the God of peace who brought again from the dead our Lord Jesus .... equip you with everything good that you may do his will......"* (Hebrews 13:20-21). *"The God of peace will be with you"* (Philippians 4:9*); "Then the God of peace will soon crush Satan under your feet"* (Romans 16: 20); *"Grace to you and peace from God our Father"* (Colossians 1:2).

God the Son is also the Eternal Peace and also the Eternal Source of Peace. The Bible says, *"Grace to you and peace from God the Father and the Lord Jesus Christ"* (11 Thessalonians 1:2); "For to us a child is born, to us a son is given; and the government will be upon his shoulder, and his name will be called *"Wonderful Counsellor, Mighty God, Everlasting Father, Prince of Peace"* (Isaiah 9:6); *"Peace I leave with you; my peace I give to you; not as the world gives do I give you. Let not your hearts be troubled, neither let them be afraid"* (John 14:27).

God the Holy Spirit is also the Eternal Peace and also the Eternal Source of Peace. The Bible says, *"For the kingdom of God is not food and drink but righteousness and peace and joy in the Holy Spirit"* (Romans 14:17).

The devil, on the other hand, is the very embodiment of restlessness. He told God that he had been *"going to and fro on the earth, and from walking up and down on it"* (Job 1:7).

Going to and fro and walking up and down can only be the way of restlessness.

2. PEACE WITH GOD

There was hostility between man and God because of man's sin. The sinner as such could not know peace. The Bible says, *"There is no peace," says the Lord, "for the wicked"* (Isaiah 48:22).

Christ came and preached peace and died to secure it. The Bible says, *"And he came and preached peace to you who were far off and peace to those who were near"* (Ephesians 2:17).

By His death on the cross, Jesus shed his blood and made peace between God and man by His blood. The Bible says, *"And through him to reconcile to himself all things, whether on earth or in heaven, making peace by the blood of his cross"* (Colossians 1:20).

Sinners who repent and receive the Lord Jesus are justified and have peace with God the Father. *"Therefore, since we are justified by faith, we have peace with God through our Lord Jesus Christ"* (Romans 5:1). The Gospel is this good news that peace has been won and sinners can now be reconciled to God (Acts 10:36). God invites men to peace with Him (Isaiah 27:5).

With regard to this Peace with God, the believer enters into it in all its fullness at conversion. He is at peace. He knows that there is no condemnation, no guilt as he stands before God. When a believer sins, his peace with God is disturbed; but when he repents, the peace is restored.

3. PEACE WITH OTHER PEOPLE

Jesus did not only bring peace between man and God. He also brought peace between man and man. Because Jesus brought peace, He is anxious that there be peace between believer and believer, and between the believer and the unbeliever. The believer, as a new creation, is commanded to seek peace with all men. The command is so imperative that we can only neglect it to our undoing.

1 Peter 3:10-11:

"For 'he that would love life and see good days, let him keep his tongue from evil and his lips from speaking guile; let him turn away from evil and do right; let him seek peace and pursue it.'"

Romans 14:19:

"Let us then pursue what makes for peace and for mutual upbuilding."

Mark 9:50:

"Have salt in yourselves, and be at peace with one another."

Romans 12:18:

"If possible, so far as it depends upon you, live peaceably with all."

Romans 12:16:

"Live in harmony with one another; do not be haughty, but associate with the lowly; never be conceited. Repay no one evil for evil, but take thought for what is noble in the sight of all."

Hebrews 12:14:

"Strive for peace with all men, and for the holiness without which no man will see the Lord."

So the believer has no choice but to do everything possible to be at peace with other believers, and even with those who are lost. Because peace does not come easily, he is to strive for peace, to seek peace, to pursue it. In some cases it may not be possible to live at peace, but in such a case the believer should make sure that he has done all he could to ensure that there is peace.

4. JESUS ALSO BROUGHT WAR

God does not want peace at any cost. He does not want peace at the price of the truth. Peace is excellent, but it must not be preferred to the truth. When a choice arises between the truth and peace, the truth must take the pre-eminence. There are times when the truth will shatter unholy peace and unholy unity and bring war. The truth must be preferred; for the Lord Jesus, the very Prince of peace said, *"Do not think that I have come to bring peace on earth; I have not come to bring peace, but a sword. For I have come to set a man against his father and a daughter against her mother, and a daughter-in-law against her mother-in-law; and a man's foes will be those of his own household"* (Matthew 10:34-36).

He further said, *"I came to cast fire upon the earth; and would that it were already kindled! I have a baptism to be baptized with; and how I am constrained until it is accomplished! Do you think that I have come to give peace on earth? No, I tell you, but rather division; for henceforth in one house there will be five divided, three against two and two against three; they will be divided, father against son and son against father, mother against daughter and daughter against her mother, mother-in-law against her daughter-in-law and daughter-in-law against her mother-in-law"* (Luke 12:49-53).

We are to follow the example of Christ and labor for peace with all men, but never compromise the truth even in the slightest way. We must never seek false peace, which is peace at the price of the truth; for God will have no part in it.

5. PERMANENT PEACE WILL BE POSSIBLE IN THE FUTURE

The Lord Jesus is going to come back in glory and power and rule on earth. During this reign there will be permanent and perfect peace on earth. The Word of God says, *"Of the increase of his government and of peace there will be no end, upon the throne of David, and over his kingdom, to establish it, and to uphold it with justice and with righteousness from this time forth and for evermore. The zeal of the Lord of hosts will do this"* (Isaiah 9:7). *"Rejoice greatly, O daughter of Zion! Shout aloud, O daughter of Jerusalem! Lo, your king comes to you; triumphant and victorious is he, humble and riding on an ass, on a colt the foal of an ass. I will cut off the chariot from Ephraim and the war horse from Jerusalem, and the battle bow shall be cut off, and he shall command peace to the nations; his dominion shall be from sea to sea, and from the River to the ends of the earth"* (Zechariah 9:9-10).

So far-reaching shall be the peace enjoyed in those days that *"The wolf shall dwell with the lamb, and the leopard shall lie down with the kid, and the calf and the lion and the fatling together, and a little child shall lead them"* (Isaiah 11:6).

This will take place when the Prince of peace rules personally. Until then, try as man may, there will be wars and rumours of war (Matthew 24:6-14).

6. THE BELIEVER'S PERSONAL PEACE

The believer's peace is inner tranquility, even amidst the mighty storms of fire. It is not the result of shallow optimism but of deep-rootedness in the Lord, the eternal God. It is the result of the deep assurance that the Lord God omnipotent reigns and cannot be overthrown. It is the result of knowing Him who is sovereign, whose purposes must stand and cannot be overthrown or thwarted.

7. THE NATURE OF THE BELIEVER'S PEACE

The believer's peace is nothing less than the peace that God the Father, the Son and the Holy Spirit possesses. The apostle Paul calls it the peace of God (Philippians 4:7) and the Lord Jesus calls it *"My peace"* (John 14:27). This peace is not only that of God. The believer's peace is nothing less than God the Son Himself. The Bible, in talking about the Lord Jesus, says, *"And he is our peace"* (Ephesians 2:14). This is most wonderful. Our peace is not only an aspect of the fruit of the Spirit, but it is also a Person, the Lord of glory. Let me say it humbly but confidently to you, *"You carry within you God's Eternal Peace, not as something but as Someone - the Lord of glory."* This is just wonderful. Words fail me to communicate on paper what l feel about it!

From the moment when a person repents towards God and has faith in the Lord Jesus, God's Eternal Peace, the Lord Jesus, takes permanent residence within him. As the person then grows in the knowledge of the Lord Jesus, he grows in the knowledge of the peace of God. The extent to which he allows Jesus to fill and possess his life is the extent to which he will be filled and possessed by the peace of God.

8. PEACE: THE BELIEVER'S LEGACY

Before the Lord left this world for His heavenly glory, He told the disciples, *"Peace I leave with you; my peace I give to you; not as the world gives do I give to you. Let not your hearts be troubled, neither let them be afraid"* (John 14:27). The Lord left His peace for us as a legacy. This peace is embodied, not in a thing, but in no one other than the Blessed Holy Spirit. He left us the Holy Spirit - His Peace. He did not give us as the world gives. How does the world give? There are three characteristics of the world's giving:

1. It depends upon merit. When the object no longer merits the gift, it is withdrawn. Unlike the world, the Lord gave us His Peace, the Holy Spirit, to be with us for ever (John 14:15), even though we do not merit Him at all.

2. It may get out of supply. The world may want to continue giving, but because of a limited supply that runs out it is not able to. This, however, is not the case with Jesus. We have God's Peace - the Holy Spirit - in abundance. *"And*

from his fulness have we all received, grace upon grace" (John 1:16), *"For it is not by measure that he gives the Spirit"* (John 3:34).

3. The gift may be there but its quality has changed with time, so much so that it can no longer satisfy. Not so with the peace of the Lord embodied in the Holy Spirit. He is unchanging.

So we have the Peace of the Lord for all time, in full supply and in unchanging quality. Do not go looking for peace as if it were something outside of you. It is there! He is there! Turn to Him. Don't allow your hearts to be troubled. Don't let fear come in. Rather, allow the Peace of God to flood you.

Further reasons why this peace is there in us is the fact that it is God's ordination for us. God has ordained peace for us. The Bible says, *"O Lord, thou wilt ordain peace for us"* (Isaiah 26:12). Peace is also a covenant of the unchanging God. The Bible says, *"For the mountains may depart and the hills be removed, but my steadfast love shall not depart from you, and my covenant of peace shall not be removed, says the Lord, who has compassion on you"* (Isaiah 54:10). This covenant of peace is based on God's love and God's compassion on us. How unsearchable are the depths of His love and compassion!

9. PEACE THAT PASSES UNDERSTANDING

The peace of God in the heart of the believer is something totally supernatural. It is completely from above. It has no grain of this world in it. It is peace inside even when there are fightings and terrors outside. An East African martyr stood before his executors. He had said goodbye to his wife and children a few hours before that moment. His executors asked, "Do you have anything to say before we shoot you?" He answered, "l have two things to say. First of all, l love you. Secondly, l want to sing for you." Then he sang for them. When he finished, he told them he was ready. They were trembling. He was calm, composed. They shot him but he went to glory, all in peace. They had guns without peace. He had Christ and peace. It is this kind of peace that God has put in His children and which He would want to be manifested at all times, regardless of circumstances. It is not outward but deeply inward. It is the product of the indwelling Holy Spirit. Another servant of God wrote after many years of imprisonment for Jesus, "l maintain my own peace." Yes, his own peace flowing daily and continuously from the indwelling Holy Spirit. How can the world understand such peace? It is beyond understanding.

As we have said, it is supernatural. It is not the result of a human philosophy or of carnal discipline. Once an elderly lady stood apparently calm in the midst of great insult. A younger girl asked her, "How is it that you manage to be so calm under such insult?" There upon she replied, "Oh daughter, you do not know how l am boiling inside." Outwardly calm but boiling inside, that is the world's peace. Ours is deep-seated and deep-rooted. It is inward calm that is manifested outwardly as the Holy Spirit takes increasing possession of the man's spirit, then his soul and, finally, his body. Such peace guards the heart. It protects it from being disturbed by what is happening outwardly. There may be tumult for the body and soul to experience. There may be pain and anguish, but the spirit is perfectly calm, protected, kept, guarded by the Holy Spirit who is the Peace of God.

What this means is that anger, wrath, quick-temperedness, a capacity for quick and violent reactions, a tendency to be easily upset, unsteadiness, a capacity for easy excitement, a touchy spirit are manifestations of the lack of deep peace and deep-rootedness in the Lord.

10.   MAINTAINING THE PEACE OF GOD

As we have seen, the Peace of God is embodied in His Son - the Lord Jesus - and made available to the believer through the Person of the Holy Spirit. There is a sense in which all believers possess the Peace of God. However, the desire of God is that peace should be maintained, experienced and enjoyed.

It is in this direction that the apostle Paul constantly prayed, yearned and wished that the saints would experience God's peace (Philippians 4:9; Titus 1:4; Colossians 1:1; 1 Timothy 1:2; 2 Timothy 1:2, etc), for what is the use to the individual of blessings that are in him but are not enjoyed by him?

The question immediately arises, How can a believer maintain and enjoy the Peace of God which is his inheritance? Below are the suggestions from the Bible:

1.   By righteousness:

All believers have the righteousness of God imputed to them. But all believers must experience righteousness. Their lives must be right with God. Sin just has to be removed and removed in every form and manifestation. Those who ensure that there is no sin in their lives will enjoy God's peace. The Psalmist says, *"Let me hear what God the Lord will speak, for he will speak peace to his people, to his saints, to those who turn to him in their hearts. Surely his salvation is at hand for those who fear him, that glory may dwell in our land. Steadfast love and faithfulness will meet; righteousness and peace will kiss each other"* (Psalm 85:8-10). *"And the effect of righteousness will be peace, and the result of righteousness quietness and trust for ever"* (Isaiah 32:17). *"He enters into peace; they rest in their beds who walk in their righteousness"* (Isaiah 57:2).

2.   By concentrating on the Lord and trusting him:

The Bible says, *"Thou dost keep him in perfect peace, whose mind is stayed on thee, because he trusts in thee"* (Isaiah 26:3). Worry is the result of taking our eyes off the Lord and concentrating on the circumstances of life. The disciple Peter was one day invited by the Lord to walk on the water to Him. Peter obeyed and, as long as he concentrated on the Lord, he walked on the water. Unfortunately, he did not keep his gaze on the Lord. He turned and fixed his gaze on the waves and immediately his faith gave way to fear and then to worry and he began to sink. Those whose minds concentrate on the Lord have no worries.

Another key to perfect peace is trusting the Lord. Proverbs says, *"Trust in the Lord with all your heart, and do not rely on your own insight. In all your ways acknowledge him, and he will make straight your paths"* (Proverbs 3:5-6). Do you trust the Lord? Do you know Him as the unfailing God? Do you know Him as the sovereign Lord whose counsel will stand? He says, *"My counsel shall stand, and I will accomplish all my purpose"* (Isaiah 46:10). He further says, *"I have spoken, and I will bring it to pass; I have purposed, and I will do it"* (Isaiah 46:11). Do you know Him as the One whose purposes cannot be thwarted? Out of deep dealings by God and with God, Job could say, *"I know that thou canst do all things, and that no purpose of thine can be thwarted"* (Job 42:2). We all need to come to the place where we, too, can say this, not only from the head but also from the heart. When you know God that way and trust Him in full assurance that nothing can happen to you without His permission, for He says, *"Are not two sparrows sold for a penny? And not one of them will fall to the ground without your Father's will. But even the hairs of your head are numbered"* (Matthew 10:29-30), then you will be at peace. Do you know that He will work out all that He permits to happen to you for your good, in order to enable you to be conformed to the image of His Son? The Bible says, *"We know that in everything God works for good with those who love him, who are called according to his purpose"* (Romans 8:28).

So there is a choice between trusting Him and being at peace, which is righteousness, or doubting Him and worrying, which is sin. He has commanded us not to worry. Please read the following aloud to yourself, then stop, thank Him and put it into practice. He says, *"Therefore I tell you, do not be anxious about your life, what you shall eat, nor about your body, what you shall put on. For your life is more than food, and the body more than clothing. Consider the ravens; they neither sow nor reap, they have neither storehouse nor barn, and yet God feeds them. Of how much more value are you than the birds! And which of you by being anxious can add a cubit to his span of life? If then you are not able to do as small a thing as that, why are you anxious about the rest? Consider the lilies, how they grow; they neither toil nor spin; yet I tell you, even Solomon in all his glory was not arrayed like one of these. But if God so clothes the grass which is alive in the field today and tomorrow is thrown into the oven, how much more will he clothe you, O men of little faith! And do not seek what you are to eat and what you are to drink, nor be of anxious mind. For all the nations of the world seek these things, and your Father knows that you need them. Instead, seek his kingdom, and these things shall be yours as well. Fear not, little flock, for it is your Father's good pleasure to give you the kingdom. Sell your possessions, and give alms; provide yourselves with purses that do not grow old, with a treasure in the heavens that does not fail, where no thief approaches and no moth destroys. For where your treasure is, there will your heart be also"* (Luke 12:22-34).

Do you see in this something which is utterly from above? In the world, people seek these things, but the children of the Kingdom, instead of seeking them, gathering and accumulating them, are to get rid of them and then be utterly rich. This is that which the world cannot understand; that which must sound to them like folly, but which is the way to the peace of God that passeth all understanding.

If your heart is still set on things: clothes, food, possessions, diplomas and all that the world offers, you cannot know the peace of God. When those things are taken away from your heart, the peace of God will replace them.

11. PEACE FOR THE LOVERS OF THE WORD

The Psalmist said, *"Great peace have those who love thy law; nothing can make them stumble"* (Psalm 119:165). And the Lord said, *"O that you had harkened to my commandments! Then your peace would have been like a river, and your righteousness like the waves of the sea"* (Isaiah 48:18).

Those who love the Word of the Lord concentrate on it, and, as they fill their being with it, great peace floods their hearts like a river. Those who fill themselves with worldly things reap out of them the worry that is so characteristic of the world. A brother gave us his radio set so that we might sell it and put the proceeds into the production of gospel tracts. He said, "Each time l listen to the news on the radio, l hear only bad news that leads to worry. l do not need it." So to read God's Word; to concentrate on it and to obey it, leads to perfect peace.

So we see that peace can result from filling our minds with the right things. The apostle says, *"Finally, brethren, whatever is honorable, whatever is just, whatever is pure, whatever is lovely, whatever is gracious, if there is any excellence, if there is anything worthy of praise, think about these things. What you have learned and received and heard and seen in me, do; and the God of peace will be with you"* (Philippians 4:8-9).

What do you concentrate your mind on? Do you fill it with evil thoughts, hatred, failure, all that will go wrong, etc? These will produce worry and distort peace.

Are your companions people at peace or people who worry? You will soon be like them, so be careful who they are. Peace is also the result of the right language. The Bible says that evil men do not speak peace (Psalm 35:20). We who are the righteous of God must speak peace and it shall flow in us and through us.

12. Peace, not laziness

Do not misunderstand peace to mean inactivity. The Lord of glory, Jesus Christ, was extremely busy. He was always on the move. If you want to catch a glimpse of how busy He was, just go away for some hours and read Mark's gospel from start to finish and you will see it for yourself. He was busy, but at peace. John Wesley was very busy, but at peace. This happens because the peace of God comes from within, it does not depend on outward activity or inactivity. Peace is not sluggishness. We are called to redeem the time. Sleeping saints are not at peace; for they are disobeying the law of the God who works. Ask God for much to do and, at the same time, let His peace flow through you.

13. GOD'S PEACE: THE REFEREE OF LIFE

The Bible says, *"And let the peace of Christ rule in your hearts, to which indeed you were called in the one body. And be thankful"* (Colossians 3:15). In a game of football, the referee controls the game. When he blows his whistle, all must stop and listen to what he has to say. Any goal scored after the referee's whistle has sounded is never counted.

The peace of God put in our hearts by the Holy Spirit is the umpire of our life and of our walk with God. When we are walking with God we have perfect peace. When there is the slightest disturbance in our inward peace, we must immediately stop and listen to the Holy Spirit, for He wants to say something. The slightest disturbance of our peace is a whistle from the umpire of life. If we do not stop and listen, we can go on, but all that we do then will be outside His will and, not only useless to Him, but opposed to His will. This presupposes that we are walking close to the Lord; for only those who walk close to Him will feel His slightest touch. Those who walk at a distance from Him will not feel His slight touches, and so will go the way of error until He has to shout to bring them to a stop.

Are you walking close to the Lord? If so, you will be led by the peace of God. Do not do anything about which you have no peace, even though you may have many logical reasons for doing it. Please, remember that the peace of God passes all understanding. It is not irrational. It is not rational. It is super-rational. It deals with the dimension in which God lives and acts.

If you have peace today but tomorrow you have no peace and the next day you have peace, you should know that you have disobeyed the Lord somewhere and that His peace is no longer ruling in you. The peace of God does not come and go. It comes from Him and becomes established through increasing prayer and fellowship with Him. The ups and downs of an unsteady life are not of God's leading. In fact, l consider them the invitation of God for you to abandon the way you are about to take.

When someone disobeys and continues in the pathway of disobedience, God will give him up and then he will have a kind of "peace" that results from the fact that the Spirit of God has ceased to strive with him. God will not strive endlessly with anyone who chooses the way of disobedience. He will strive up to a point, then He will let the person go. From that point on the person will have peace, but it will be false peace.

I well remember a sister who wanted to marry an unbeliever. She was told not to do so. She persisted with the relationship. After some time, she said, "l used to pray about this matter and would have no peace about it. But now l have peace to go on." Yes, she had "peace," but not God's peace. She will end, not in peace, but in pieces. You who are going on the way of disobedience, do you have God's peace or the peace that will soon become pieces?

As we saw in the verse, the peace that rules in the obedient heart is the peace that calls us into the body of Christ. When you are out of fellowship with the body of Christ expressed in a local assembly, and disagree with that body, whatever you have is very likely to be false peace. So, brethren, the peace is inward but it also operates in the context of the body of Christ.

14. FINALLY

Permanent peace is the result of permanent rest in the Lord. It is the result of utter abandonment to Him. *"So then, there remains a sabbath rest for the people of God; for whoever enters God's rest also ceases from his labours as God did from his. Let us therefore strive to enter that rest"* (Hebrews 4:9-11). Let us cease from our own labours, the labours of our own making, and let us enter into the rest of God and give God the opportunity to work His works through us and, then, we shall be truly at peace. Glory be to His holy Name!

Patience and long-suffering (endurance)

Patience is the spiritual capacity of being slow to anger; the capacity to be able to wait with a restful spirit. Long-suffering includes the capacity to bear with the unbearable; the capacity not to react immediately in the face of great insult. Patience and long-suffering are characteristics of lives in which the Holy Spirit has done a deep work of humbling, breaking and remoulding. All who have walked with God for considerable lengths of time come to a knowledge of Him as the God of all-patience and long-suffering, and He makes them like Himself - patient and long-suffering.

1. THE PATIENCE OF GOD AND HIS LONG-SUFFERING

The patience of God is not a resignation to the inevitable; for there is nothing inevitable as far as He is concerned. His patience is an active and purposeful force. He is patient, so that people may have the time and the opportunity to come to repentance and salvation.

When God introduced Himself to Moses, He said, *"The Lord, the Lord, a God merciful and gracious, slow to anger, and abounding in steadfast love and faithfulness"* (Exodus 34:6). He was patient and long-suffering with the children of Israel. The Bible says, *"Their heart was not steadfast towards him; they were not true to his covenant. Yet he, being compassionate, forgave their iniquity, and did not destroy them; he restrained his anger often, and did not stir up all his wrath. He remembered that they were but flesh, a wind that passes and comes not again. How often they rebelled against him in the wilderness and grieved him in the desert! They tested him again and again, and provoked the Holy One of Israel"* (Psalm 78:37-41).

This passage tells us so much about the patience and long-suffering of God with the children of Israel (His people) that we must draw a few lessons from it.

First of all, the object of His patience. These were people who knew His goodness and power towards them and had promised to walk with Him, but their heart was not steadfast towards Him; they were not true to His covenant. They rebelled against Him often. They grieved Him. They tested Him again and again. They provoked Him.

What they deserved was judgment - immediate and severe judgment. They earned it by constant sin and rebellion, yet these people were the object of His patience and long-suffering love.

Secondly, we see the attributes of God that made it possible for Him to be patient with them. These attributes include:

a. His mercy.

b. His graciousness.

c. His steadfast love that abounds.

d. His compassion.

e. His capacity to forgive.

In addition to those attributes, God actively did the following:

a. He restrained His anger often.

b. He did not stir up all His wrath.

Thirdly, God remembered what they were. They were:

a. but flesh

b. a wind that passes and comes not again.

The result of all these is that He did not destroy them, but allowed them to go and inherit the Promised Land.

The same message goes out through the entire Bible. The Psalmist said, *"He made known his ways to Moses, his acts to the people of Israel. The Lord is merciful and gracious, slow to anger and abounding in steadfast love. He will not always chide, nor will he keep his anger for ever. He does not deal with us according to our sins, nor requite us according to our iniquities. For as the heavens are high above the earth, so great is his steadfast love toward those who fear him; as far as the east is from the west, so far does he remove our transgressions from us. As a father pities his children, so the Lord pities those who fear him. For he knows our frame; he remembers that we are dust"* (Psalm 103:7-14).

Jonah could complain and say, *"For I knew that thou art a gracious God and merciful, slow to anger, and abounding in steadfast love, and repentest of evil"* (Jonah 4:2). Yes, our God is great. Let us, with the Psalmist, say, *"But thou, O Lord, art a God merciful and gracious, slow to anger and abounding in steadfast love and faithfulness. Turn to me and take pity on me; give thy strength to thy servant, and save the son of thy handmaid. Show me a sign of thy favour, that those who hate me may see and be put to shame because thou, Lord, hast helped me and comforted me"* (Psalm 86:15-17).

2. THE PATIENCE OF GOD WITH THE UNSAVED

The Bible says, *"The Lord is not slow about his promise as some count slowness, but is forbearing toward you, not wishing that any should perish, but that all should reach repentance"* (2 Peter 3:9). Yes, His patience is purposeful. The apostle asked, *"Or do you presume upon the riches of his kindness and forbearance and patience? Do you not know that God's kindness is meant to lead you to repentance?"* (Romans 2:4). This patience of God with unbelievers is wonderful. I know it; for He was patient towards me.

3. THE PATIENCE OF GOD WITH HARDENED SINNERS

There comes a point in the life of the one who rejects the Lord Jesus when he says his final, "No," to God and the Holy Spirit gives him up. From that moment, he becomes a hardened sinner, *"a vessel of wrath made for destruction"* (Romans 9:22). Yet God does not destroy such immediately. It would be alright if He judged such at once and cast them into the lake of fire. Rather, He *"has endured with much patience the vessel of wrath made for destruction"* (Romans 9:22).

4. THE PATIENCE OF THE LORD JESUS WITH THE UNSAVED

Here Paul is the classic example. He himself writes and says, *"The saying is sure and worthy of full acceptance, that Christ Jesus came into the world to save sinners. And I am the foremost of sinners; but I received mercy for this reason, that in me, as the foremost, Jesus Christ might display his perfect patience for an example to those who were to believe in him for eternal life"* (1 Timothy 1:15-16).

Jesus was not only patient with Paul, He was patient with the twelve in their hardness of heart, their slowness in understanding and the smallness of their faith. He was patient with them as they struggled for earthly, instead of heavenly greatness. He was patient with them as they hardly understood that He must die and then rise again.

He was patient with Peter who first promised to be faithful, then denied Him completely. Yet His love and patience reached out to him, forgave him, restored him and made him the leading apostle.

He was patient with Judas whom He knew from the beginning would betray Him, yet He appointed him to a high office and loved him right to the night of the betrayal. He is indeed patience incarnate.

5. THE PATIENCE OF THE LORD WITH THE ELECT

How often the Lord has been patient with me! In my many failures He has been patient. How patient He has been with the Church! In her ignorance, sin, lovelessness, division, worldliness, etc, the Lord has stood by her, cleansing, purifying, sanctifying and making her ready for Himself. This is wonderful. Where would we be were He not patient with us?

6. THE PATIENCE OF THE BELIEVER

The Lord God has imparted His patience to the believer. In a sense, all believers have the patience of God as an inheritance. God, however, is concerned that the believer enter into the enjoyment of his inheritance. Thus, the believer, although possessing the patience of God, must experience it day by day. The exhortation to be patient must be seen as an invitation to enter into the fullness of patience and not an invitation to seek something from the outside; for God has given the believer Christ and in Him all the treasures of God are hidden. Those who pursue Christ will enter into the enjoyment of these treasures, including patience and long-suffering.

7. THE COMMAND TO BE PATIENT

The Bible says, *"May you be strengthened with all power, according to his glorious might, for all endurance and patience with joy"* (Colossians 1:11). *"And we exhort you, brethren, admonish the idlers, encourage the fainthearted, help the weak, be patient with them all"* (1 Thessalonians 5:14).

Because the command is given, it must be obeyed. Impatience is disobedience. It is sin.

8. THE BELIEVER : PATIENT WITH GOD AND WITH CIRCUMSTANCES

The believer must be patient with God. He has made many wonderful promises in His Word and He will fulfil all of them. However, He will not fulfil them according to our plans and our timing. He will fulfil them according to His timing. All who know Him must wait on Him. If He has not yet acted, it must be that the time has not yet come. The Lord Jesus said to His mother, "O woman, what have you to do with me? My hour has not yet come" (John 2:4). Do you wait for His timing? Joseph received a revelation that his parents and brethren would bow to him. That was God's fact. Nothing could change it, yet it took very many years and much suffering to bring that to pass. These were years of severe testing. Thanks be to God that Joseph was patient with God and with circumstances! Sometimes many believers act as if God were too slow. They make their plans and say, "By this year I should have accomplished this or that." Then God brings His own plans and, while He is working them out, they complain. One of the worst sins against God is complaining and questioning Him. This is the product of severe impatience. It is also the manifestation of an unsurrendered heart. Jesus told the unbelieving Jews that His time had not yet come although their time was always there. Does He say the same to you? All who are impatient with God go wrong unless they repent deeply.

The answer to a heart that is impatient with God is full and unreserved surrender to Him. Where that surrender has taken place, the heart rests in God and there is peace and patience.

What about circumstances? God is the Lord of all circumstances. The fully yielded rest in Him. Instead of fighting, they rest and enjoy God's peace and are patient even with unfavourable circumstances; for He alone can change them.

9. THE BELIEVER: PATIENT WITH OTHER BELIEVERS

Any believer who is impatient with the faults of another is foolish. Do you remember how patient the Lord has been with you? Do you remember how many times He has picked you up? Do you remember some lessons which He had to teach you over and over and then you now behave as if you were perfect from the very beginning?

Those who believe the Lord deeply have faith in Him and in His purposes. They also have faith that He will bring all His elect to perfection. Having such faith, they are patient with the elect who are being perfected.

A threefold treatment of impatience with other believers is:

1. Remember how God has been patient with you.
2. Remember that God will perfect them; that they are servants of another and, as such, it is not your business to be impatient with them.
3. Remember that patience will help you, whereas impatience will destroy them and you!

10. THE BELIEVER: PATIENT WITH UNBELIEVERS

The Lord of glory was patient with unbelievers. He was patient even with Judas Iscariot and loved him right unto the end. The disciple must follow suit. He must be patient with all unbelievers, regardless of their attitude to the Lord of glory, the Gospel, the Bible or the believer. He must be patient with them in their blindness, rebellion, etc. The thought that sometimes flashes into my mind that God should destroy in one flash, all who oppose Him, is a revelation of my spiritual bankruptcy. Father, have mercy on me!

The believer must be patient with them in their sin and failure, for this will lead to their seeing the Lord and, by His grace, repenting towards God and coming to Him. We must be patient with their habits. The attitude of the believer who enters a taxi and frowns on all who are inside because they are smoking cigarettes is more an exhibition of self-righteousness than Christlikeness. The unbeliever is lost. Why do we expect him not to smoke? That is the only satisfaction he knows, dare we take it away from him before we have given him the One who satisfies?

A true story is told of a believer who, as a student, shared a room with an unbeliever. The unbeliever was not interested in the Gospel. He loved sin. Every Friday night , he would go out and get drunk, then come home and vomit on the floor of their room. The believer would quietly clean the vomit and wash the floor without complaining. This continued every Friday for one, two, three, four, five and six months. During all these months the unbeliever got drunk and vomited and the believer cleaned the vomit without complaining. The believer also maintained a warm, loving attitude towards the unbeliever and did not allow his wicked habit to come between them. At the end of six months the unbeliever broke down and gave his life to the Lord Jesus Christ. He was overcome and shocked to conversion by the believer's love and patience. His patience did what thousands of sermons could not do.

Have you given up your unbelieving husband, wife, boss, etc, because you have prayed for them for some time and yet they have apparently become worse with increasing prayer and passing time? Stop. Repent of having given them up. The Lord has not given them up. The Bible says, *"The Lord is not slow about his promise as some count slowness, but is forbearing toward you, not wishing that any should perish, but that all should reach repentance"* (2 Peter 3:9). The Lord is forbearing. He is long-suffering. Be like him. Be patient with them and pray them through to salvation.

Have you ever thought about the fact that God has been very patient with you?

11. THE BELIEVER: PATIENT WITH HIMSELF

One proverb says, "Rome was not built in one day," and another, "The heights which great men reached and maintained were not attained by sudden flight but, while their companions slept, they kept toiling upward in the sky." You will not become a spiritual giant overnight. You are being changed gradually into His likeness. The Bible says, *"And we all, with unveiled face, beholding the glory of the Lord, are being changed into his likeness from one degree of glory to another; for this comes from the Lord who is the Spirit"* (11 Corinthians 3:18). Be patient with yourself. If you are faithful in following the Lord, you can trust your progress into His hands. He knows what He is doing. Worry and depression over the fact that you have made so little progress after many years in the Lord can only hinder further progress. Relax. The Lord is not slow concerning His promise to bring you to perfection. Have confidence in Him; for He who began a good work in you will bring it to completion. As you confide in Him, be patient with yourself.

12. PATIENT WITH JOY AND WITHOUT COMPLAINING

There will always be things that will come out to attempt to make the believer impatient. He may have to face many contradictions in himself and around. He may be insulted and maltreated, yet he is to wait on God and not act in the place of God. The question is, "How is he to wait? How is he to bear the wrong inflicted on him? He may be persecuted. How should he react? There are five possible attitudes:

1. He could be impatient and manifest it. This would be sin.
2. He could be impatient and not manifest it. This, too, would be sin before God.
3. He could just bear it with grumbling. This, too, would be sin.
4. He could bear it calmly.
5. He could bear it and manifest patience with joy. This is Christlike.

The Bible says, *"Do all things without grumbling or questioning, that you may be blameless and innocent, children of God without blemish in the midst of a crooked and perverse generation, among whom you shine as lights in the world"* (Philippians 2:14). Patience is the capacity to endure with joy. You must not only be patient, but you must be patient with joy. There should be a spontaneous song of praise flowing from your heart to the

Lord when you face those trying circumstances that require patience. *"May you be strengthened with all power, according to his glorious might, for all endurance and patience with joy"* (Colossians 1:11).

13. THE MARKS OF THE PATIENT

Those who are patient at heart, that is, those in whose life the Lord has worked out His patience, will manifest it by the following characteristics:

1. Sympathy towards all men
2. Tender-heartedness
3. Humility
4. Forgiveness
5. Graciousness
6. Compassion
7. Restrained anger.

The patient of heart are patient under all circumstances. They are patient with:

1. The clumsy
2. Slow-thinkers and slow speakers and actors
3. The dim-witted
4. Fools
5. All men, as the Bible says, *"We exhort you, brethren, admonish the idlers, encourage the fainthearted, help the weak, be patient with them all"* (1 Thessalonians 5:14).

14. THE MARKS OF THE IMPATIENT

The impatient, that is, those in whom the cross has not been allowed to do a deep work in this dimension, will manifest the following characteristics of the old nature:

1. Quick temper
2. A touchy spirit
3. A capacity to flare up
4. Wrath
5. Insolence, and the like
6. An unforgiving attitude.

15. PATIENCE: A SPIRITUAL CONDITION

True patience in the terms we are using is not some natural characteristic. It is not some superficial trait. It is something that has its home in the spirit of man and its origin in the Holy Spirit. The Bible says, *"The patient in spirit is better than the proud in spirit"* (Ecclesiastes 7:8). Natural tolerance will give way under trying circumstances, but patience that has been worked out by the Holy Spirit and made a part of the heart-condition of the saint who has suffered, is permanent.

16. HOW TO BE PATIENT

The Cross of Christ must bring all the manifestations of impatience listed above to an end. The believer must confess each one of them as deep sin. These are manifestations of the devil's character. Therefore, the believer must hate them with the same hatred with which he hates stealing, killing, adultery, and the like. The cross will be greatly limited in its work when such hatred is lacking, for why should God proceed to separate a person from that which he loves?

Patience is worked out in us by the Holy Spirit. The Bible says, *"More than that, we rejoice in our sufferings, knowing that suffering produces endurance, and endurance produces character, and character produces hope"* (Romans 5:3,4). The Holy Spirit does not pour something out of heaven into us called patience. He produces patience in us by a difficult route - the way of suffering. He will allow you to suffer and to suffer very much and often very unduly. The more you suffer without complaining, the more patience will be imparted into your inner man. The more a person suffers, the more the fruit of patience will mature in him; but the less he suffers, the less patient he will be.

Many saints pray and say, "Lord give me patience." They expect God to perform magic and in one go make them patient. God can do that, but He has chosen not to. Such believers should instead pray, "Lord, grant me to be one with You in Your suffering. Make me suffer. Stand in my way a million times. Bring me to the end of my own devices." If they pray that way, they should trust God to bring them to suffer. They should not only ask, they should plead with God that their prayer be answered soon. God will answer them and bring them much suffering.

If they suffer with a complaining heart, the suffering will be of no use and they will remain impatient. If they just resign to the suffering and say,"Well, what can I do? God is greater than I, I give in," they will suffer and their suffering will produce no fruit. If they accept the suffering with thanksgiving and say to God, "Thank You for this gift of suffering which You have sent to me so that it may produce patience in me. I receive it from Your hand with love and joy, knowing that it is for my good," they will suffer and suffering will produce much patience.

1. Patience and character

The Bible says that patience produces character (Romans 5:4). The character of Christ is produced through patient suffering. This means that the impatient are off the rails of Christian character. It also means that those who run away from suffering run away from character.

It becomes imperative for every child of God to put on the patience of Christ. It becomes a must for every child of God to suffer. This means that the greatest gift that God can give any believer, next only to His precious Son, is suffering.

This means that believers should covet suffering, trials, persecutions, etc, and rejoice in them; for they are among God's greatest gifts. He who has an ear to hear, let him hear!

God bless you!!

Generosity and gratitude

1. GENEROSITY

The Bible says of the early Church in Jerusalem: *"And day by day, attending the temple together and breaking bread in their homes, they partook of food with glad and generous hearts"* (Acts 2:46).

The rich in the Church are instructed *"To do good, to be rich in good deeds, to be liberal and generous, thus laying up for themselves a good foundation for the future, so that they may take hold of the life which is life indeed"* (1 Timothy 6:18-19).

The Psalmist says, *"It is well with the man who deals generously and lends, who conducts his affairs with justice...... He has distributed freely, he has given to the poor; his righteousness endures forever, his horn is exalted in honour"* (Psalm 112:5-9).

Generosity is the spirit which gives and gives without counting what it is costing to give and rejoices, not in piling things for itself, but in seeing the needs of others met. Generosity is the giving that exceeds the normal bounds.

1.　God's generosity

God is very generous. He is always giving. He gives to the undeserving. When we were without hope, hostile to Him, He gave His Son Jesus to die for the most undeserving. When sinners crucified His Son, He nevertheless gave His Holy Spirit to those who rejected His Son and murdered Him. God has not only given us what we need. He has always given us in excess of what we need. He has always gone out of His way to ensure that His children have more than they need. How can I explain this? Let us put it this way. Suppose that I am going on a journey and my fare is ten dollars. I can ask for ten dollars. A responsible person will give me ten dollars and this amount will be sufficient. Now, if instead of the ten dollars, I am given fifty dollars, saying that it is more comfortable to travel first class and so I should pay more and enjoy the comforts of the first class and that, in addition, I need some extra money so that if my ticket is lost, I may be able to buy another one and that I do not need to walk from the train station to the house but I should hire a taxi, or, if in addition, I am told that in order to present the best image of myself I should buy some gift for the people I am going to and that, although those people will supply all my needs, I need pocket money and money for any emergencies, then I have been treated generously. Ten dollars could meet the basic need, but the wants and wishes were supplied. That is generosity, and God always treats us with generosity.

The Bible says that God's generosity extends even to the wicked, *"For he makes his sun rise on the evil and on the good, and sends rain on the just and on the unjust"* (Matthew 5:45).

2.   The way to generosity

Generosity is the mark of those in whose lives God has done three basic things:

1. Given them a profound desire to conform to Him. Because such people see Him as the all-generous God, they follow in His steps.

2. Delivered them from the power of possessing, calculating and hoarding. Without this deliverance, people would always be asking, *"What is the minimum that I can give to meet his needs?"* When the deliverance has been accomplished, the person asks, *"What is the maximum that I can give to meet his needs?"*

3. Had their eyes opened to consider the needs of the other person and not just their personal needs. Such a person, if he had one hundred thousand francs and someone needed ten thousand for, say, medical care, he would not just give the ten thousand francs and go away satisfied. He would consider that if the treatment requires ten thousand francs, it is possible that the person in need may not also have transport money, food money, etc. He will, therefore, not only give the required ten thousand but will give something in excess of that.

The goal of the generous is not just to meet the basic needs but to go beyond those needs; to give as God gives. We can ask, "How does God give?"

3.   The God of limitless abundance and generosity

God is limitless in His generosity. The Bible says, *"Now to him who by the power at work within us is able to do far more abundantly than all that we ask or think, to him be glory in the church and in Christ Jesus to all generations, for ever and ever. Amen"* (Ephesians 3:20-21). We can write this out this way:

- 500 … God gives far more abundantly than we ask or think.
- 400 … God gives more abundantly than we ask or think.
- 300 … God gives abundantly what we ask or think.
- 200 … What we think we ought to have but do not have the courage to ask.
- 100 … What we actually ask and hope.
- 0 … The place where we are when we begin to ask God.

Even after God has given us so much, He still has more in store to give. Luke expresses the same thing in the following words: *"Give and it will be given to you; good measure, pressed down, shaken together, running over, will be put into your lap"* (Luke 6:38).

- 500 … All is filled and running over so that there is super over-abundance.
- 400 … That which is pressed down is shaken together to create even more room.
- 300 … The good measure is pressed down to make room for more.
- 200 … You are given what you asked in good measure.
- 100 … You are given what you asked for.
- 0 … The point where we are at the point of asking.

4.   Generous forgiveness

The Lord God also forgives in a most generous way. He is the One who is most wronged. He is the One who is wronged repeatedly, yet how generous He is in forgiving! The Bible says, *"As far as the east is from the west, so far does he remove our transgressions from us. As a father pities his children, so the Lord pities those who fear him"* (Psalm 103:12-13). *"Who is a God like thee, pardoning iniquity and passing over transgression for the remnant of his inheritance? He does not retain his anger for ever because he delights in steadfast love. He will again have compassion on us, he will tread our iniquities under foot. Thou wilt cast all our sins into the depths of the sea"* (Micah 7:18-19).

A generous heart forgives and forgives completely. It does not only forgive but it restores all the rights that were lost by sin. l will never cease to marvel at the generosity of the Lord to Peter. Peter denied Him thrice, forsook the fishing of men for the fishing of fish. The generous Jesus forgave him even before he asked for it and restored him and went ahead and made him the leader of the apostles, just as if he had been faithful all the way. This is most wonderful.

When someone says, "l will forgive but l will not forget," that one knows nothing of generosity. When a person says,"l will forgive him but l will never trust him," or "l will forgive him but keep my distance," or "l will forgive him but my confidence in him is gone for ever," he is just saying that he is not generous at all.

5.   The life of generosity

We have said that the generous give and give and give. l want to add that the generous are always giving. They give to all - the poor and the rich alike. l used to think that one should only give to those who are obviously in need, until the Lord sent a sister my way whose life of giving taught me a lot. She gave to all and at one time, even though l earn a big salary, she sent a money gift to me as a contribution to a building project that l had on. What she gave cost her a lot, although it was negligible compared to the sums of money that were being put into the project. Her gift touched my heart and ministered not so much to my material need as to my spiritual need. The small sum of money and the letter that came with it caused something to flow from the Lord to me, and my heart was warmed towards the Lord in a new way. By her material gift, she reached out and met my spiritual need in a way that a thousand sermons could not have done. l will always remember her and her generosity.

Some think that generosity is something for the rich. It is indeed something for the rich: those who are rich in the Lord. Such people who are filled with the Lord hold nothing back. They give everything away, yet they are satisfied because, like Levi of old, they own no inheritance. The Lord is their Inheritance. Such an example was the woman who gave her last two coins. She gave all she had and, as the last coins were given away, l believe that God entered into her life in a fuller measure and she became rich in God. Who can be rich in God and lack anything? Those who are poor in the Lord, even if they have all the wealth in the world, are prone to being stingy.

6.   The blessing of generosity

The Bible says, *"All day long the wicked covets, but the righteous gives and does not hold back"* (Proverbs 21:26*). "One man gives freely, yet grows all the richer; another withholds what he should give, and only suffers want"* (Proverbs 11:24). *"A liberal man will be* *enriched, and one who waters will himself be watered"* (Proverbs 11:25).

"God is able to provide you with every blessing in abundance, so that you may always have enough of everything and may provide in abundance for every good work. As it is written,

'He scatters abroad, he gives to the poor;

His righteousness endures for ever.'

He who supplies seed to the sower and bread for food will supply and multiply your resources and increase the harvest of your righteousness (benevolence). You will be enriched in every way for great generosity, which through us will produce thanksgiving to God; for the rendering of this service not only supplies the wants of the saints but also overflows in many thanksgivings to God. Under the test of this service, you will glorify God by your obedience in acknowledging the gospel of Christ, and by the generosity of your contribution for them and for all other; while they long for you and pray for you, because of the surpassing grace of God in you. Thanks be to God for this inexpressible gift" (2 Corinthians 9:8-15).

The blessings of generosity include:

1. God providing the generous with every blessing in abundance.
2. God multiplying their resources.
3. God increasing the harvest of their righteousness.
4. They will be enriched in every way.
5. They will cause many to thank God.
6. The need of others will be met.
7. God will be glorified.
8. Other believers will long for them and pray for them.

God, may all of Your children become generous!   Amen.

9.   Gratitude

Gratitude is an expression of indebtedness. It comes from a heart that knows that it does not deserve what it has. It is the acknowledgement that someone has done something for you which he was not obliged to do, and that acknowledgement is expressed.

10.   Jesus the supreme example

The Lord Jesus prayed, saying, *"I thank thee, Father, Lord of heaven and earth, that thou hast hidden these things from the wise and understanding and revealed them to babes; yea, Father, for such was thy gracious will"* (Matthew 11:25-26). On another occasion, the Saviour prayed, *"Father, I thank thee that thou hast heard me"* (John 11:41).

The Lord Jesus was the very God of very God, but from the moment when He decided to forgo all the glory of heaven and come down to earth as man, He lost all rights to anything in heaven. He then became totally dependent on the good will of the Father. So, when the Father hid things from those who thought themselves wise and revealed them to babes, the Lord Jesus was grateful for this and thanked His Father for it. God's will was being brought to pass and, since the commitment of the Lord Jesus was to see the will of God accomplished, He thanked the Father for it. Then Jesus thanked the Father for hearing Him. It is as if He was saying, "Father, I have no right to be heard, but You have nevertheless heard Me. I am grateful to You for this. Thank You." He did not express the gratitude silently. He expressed it aloud. He said it so that others might hear Him and know His heart's attitude about the matter.

The gratitude of the Lord Jesus was an expression of humility. He was expressing dependence. He was saying, "I have no right to this." He was not competing with God. He was meek and lowly of heart. Gratitude is a quality of character often found among the meek and lowly of heart. The proud of heart, who are an abomination to the Lord, are not grateful.

11. Jesus demands gratitude

The Bible says, *"And as he entered a village, he was met by ten lepers, who stood at a distance and lifted up their voices and said, 'Jesus, Master, have mercy on us.' When he saw them he said to them, 'Go and show yourselves to the priests.' And as they went they were cleansed. Then one of them, when he saw that he was healed, turned back, praising God with a loud voice; and he fell on his face at Jesus' feet, giving him thanks. Now he was a Samaritan. Then said Jesus, 'Were not ten cleansed? Where are the nine? Was no one found to return and give praise to God except this foreigner?' And he said to him, 'Rise and go your way; your faith has made you well'"* (Luke 17:12-19).

These lepers were in desperate need. The Lord was not obliged to heal them. When they cried to Him, He had mercy on them and healed them. Nine of them were Jews. One was a Samaritan. The Jews took their healing for granted. They sort of said, "He has only done His job." Or they forgot the one who healed them in the joy of their newly found freedom. They wanted the healing. They had no place for the Healer. They forgot Him. They had no time for Him. The Samaritan was different. When he found that he had been healed, his thoughts went away from himself to the One who had healed him. He turned back and went towards Jesus. His whole being was full of praise. He praised God with a loud voice. He fell on his face before the Lord Jesus. He fell at His feet. He was humble to the core. He did not only fall at His feet. He gave thanks. The Lord gave him spiritual health in addition to the physical health that he already possessed. He was doubly blessed.

The Lord wondered why the others had not come to give thanks. His heart must have ached at the fact that, by not coming back, they lost the greater healing. Had they come back, they would have each received a bonus - eternal life. But by being ungrateful, they lost it all.

12.   The believer's attitude

The believer owes a double debt of gratitude to the Lord. He owes God gratitude as the Creator and Sustainer of human life, and he owes God gratitude as the Creator and Sustainer of the New Life.

All believers must thank God for:

1. Creating them
2. All that He has given to keep life going:
   a. Fresh air
   b. Food
   c. Housing
   d. Clothing
   e. Neighbours
   f. Transportation
   g. Friends

h. Family

i. Etc.

To complain about the weather, climate, etc, is to question God in His sovereignty as the Creator. Some people complain when it is hot and complain when it is cold; they complain when it is dry and again when it is wet. This is most sad. No child of God dares put on such an attitude.

When did you last thank God for creating you and for all that He has given you to sustain your life? Is it just words like "Thank You, Lord," or is your whole being grateful?

If you are deeply grateful, your whole attitude to life will change radically. First of all, you will not complain. You will not compare yourself positively or negatively with any other person. You will consider yourself as a distinct individual put into God's world to enjoy it. You will look at each new day as a big gift from God with good works planned from the very foundation of the world for you to fill it with. You will consider every minute a blessing, every flower a gift from God, to beautify His world for your enjoyment. You will look at each human being as a potential heir of God's glorious Kingdom and, therefore, thank God for him or her. You will regard every opportunity as a manifestation of God's sovereign will and for all these things, there will go up from your lips unceasing praise.

Secondly, you will not run away from difficult situations. You will thank Him for them and do all in your power to co-operate with Him to have the situation go His way.

Thirdly, you will not complain about your size, family, nation, etc. You will thank God for all of these, since they are all part of the gracious will of a loving Father. You will say with the Lord, "I thank thee, Father..... for such was thy gracious will."

The believer will, above all, thank the Lord for the New Life in the Lord Jesus. Think about it for a moment. Are you grateful to the Lord about your salvation? Has it truly dawned on you what it would mean to be without Christ and be bound for hell? Do you know what it means to live with the wrath of God abiding on you? Do you know what it means to be bound by sin and subject to all the whims and pleasures of the wicked one? If you know these and the other terrible things that are the lot of those without Christ, you should be grateful to God for saving you.

Have you been blessed in knowing the Lord Jesus personally? Have you been blessed in being a child of God and knowing that you are an heir to the promises and the throne of God? Have you been blessed in enjoying the peace and favour of God the Father? Has it satisfied your heart in knowing that the Holy Spirit dwells in you? Have you ever seen the privileged position which God has given you in Christ Jesus by allowing you to serve Him and be a co-worker with Him in carrying out the most important job on earth? Have you ever come to grips with the privilege that God has given you in making you belong to His household? If these and the multitude of other privileges that are yours in the Lord ever dawn on you, your heart will rise in continuous and spontaneous gratitude to God.

The sad thing is that many believers take their salvation so lightly. Sometimes they make as if God made a mistake in saving them. They grumble and speak of the limitations of the Christian walk as if to say to God, "God, why did You save me? My life would have been more satisfying had You not interfered." They complain about other brethren as if to say to God, "Why did You not leave me in the world? I found unbelievers more agreeable and their companionship more satisfying." Many believers complain about God's will for their lives as if to say, "God, I would have made better plans for my life than the ones You have made for me." They complain about this and that and the other as if to say, in the final analysis, "God, You have messed my life for me, but since You are greater than I am, I bow to You; for, what can I do?"

Such an attitude of life betrays profound ingratitude. It is also a mark of pride, spiritual blindness, contempt at God, taking God's gift for granted.

If that is your heart's attitude, you can say, "Praise the Lord. Thank You, Father," at moments of passing happiness but, such praise and thanksgiving being momentary, cannot please God. Those who know their God know that He cannot err. They know that all that He does is correct, and that, as long as they love Him, He will work out all for their best interest to make them like the Lord Jesus. Such then follow the injunctions of Scripture which say,

1. *"Give thanks in all circumstances; for this is the will of God in Christ Jesus for you"* (1 Thessalonians 5:18).
2. *"He who brings thanksgiving as his sacrifice honours me"* (Psalm 50:23)...
3. *"I will give to the Lord the thanks due to his righteousness, and I will sing praises to the name of the Lord, the Most High"* (Psalm 7:17).
4. *"I will offer to thee the sacrifice of thanksgiving and call on the name of the Lord"* (Psalm 116:17).

5. *"Through him then let us continually offer up a sacrifice of praise to God, that is, the fruit of lips that acknowledge his name"* (Hebrews 13:15).

They will join the apostle Paul in thanking the Lord for all the brethren, for he thanked God, saying:

1. *"I give thanks to God always for you because of the grace of God which was given you in Christ Jesus"* (1 Corinthians 1:4). This thanksgiving was made not because of a "perfect" Church, for the Corinthians were far from that.

2. *"I thank my God in all my remembrance of you"* (Philippians 1:3)

3. *"We give thanks to God always for you all"* (1 Thessalonians 1:2).

Have you ever thanked the Lord for each believer? Not to do so would be to say that that one is so bad that it would be better for him, for you, for the world, for the cause of the Gospel if he were never a believer. It would be to say that God made a mistake in ordaining him unto eternal life and that the Holy Spirit was wrong to convict, convince and convert him. Can you take such an attitude?

13.   Gratitude to others

Those who are grateful to the Lord will also be grateful for each thing that they receive from God's creatures and from God's children. They will be grateful for all the things, both big and small. They will be grateful for kindness shown to them in every way. They will be grateful for visits, for words of encouragement, for gifts, for food, for anything that is done for them. They will constantly say, "Thank you," not lightly, but because in their innermost hearts they are grateful. In response they will do all they can to do the same to some others. The gratitude will be without partiality - it will go to all men and for all gifts, big or small. It will be expressed in "Thank you, my dear brother," or "Thank you, my dear sister." "Thank you" will not just be mere empty words, but their whole being will be allowed to flow to the Lord and to the person.

The grateful will be personal. They will not receive a gift from someone and just say, "Thanks be to God." They will say to the person who has been used by the Lord to give the gift, "Thank you for this gift." The grateful will look for ways to truly express their gratitude.

I find people who are stingy and thoughtless hurting people by their words. For example, many will receive a gift and say, "Thanks." They should have said, "Thank you very much, my dear brother." Even when the gift meets the needs of many they will rather keep quiet about it, but those who have learnt a lot from the Lord say, "Thank you again for the gift. It met my need in this or that way."

Gratitude is thus the fruit of great cultivation. You do not find it on barren spiritual trees. Are you one such? Begin today and do something about it. You will become increasingly and spontaneously grateful as you go deeper with the Lord. l suggest that while the Holy Spirit is working that out, you apply yourself in a disciplined way, to the task of putting on gratitude as follows:

1. Write out in an exercise book that has been set aside for that purpose, one thousand things about which you are grateful to God.

2. Write fifty letters of gratitude to people who have been a blessing to you, but to whom you have never clearly shown appreciation of what they did to you.

3. Day by day, open your eyes and your entire personality to situations in which you can say, "Thank You, Lord" and, also, "Thank you, Mr/ Mrs/ Miss..."

14. Finally

The grateful leper received a bonus of healing. Make gratitude your way of life and you will receive bonuses from the Lord and from those He created.

God bless you!

Humility, meekness, and lowliness

1. JESUS THE SUPREME EXAMPLE

The Lord Jesus is the supreme example of humility, meekness and lowliness. The apostle Paul said, *"Do nothing from selfishness or conceit, but in humility count others better than yourselves. Let each of you look not only to his own interests, but also to the interests of others. Have this mind among yourselves, which is yours in Christ Jesus, who, though He was in the form of God, did not count equality with God a thing to be grasped, but emptied himself, taking the form of a servant, being born in the likeness of men. And being found in human form he humbled himself and became obedient unto death, even death on a cross. Therefore God has highly exalted him and bestowed on him the name which is above every name, that at the name of Jesus every knee should bow, in heaven and on earth and under the earth, and every tongue confess that Jesus Christ is Lord, to the glory of God the Father"* (Philippians 2:3-11).

The Lord Jesus took seven steps into absolute degradation, all of them a manifestation of His humility and His love.

1. He consecrated Himself to humility. He did this by recognizing who He was. He was in the form of God

and He knew it. He was equal to God and He knew it. He was God and He knew this fact too. Had He stayed in heaven and just proclaimed the fact that He was God, He would not have been lying at all. He had all His rights and all His glory and position as God. He was indeed exalted! However, He did not count equality with God as a thing to be grasped. He did not insist on that which was His by right. He was willing to take the second place, the place of the Son, and accept all the limitations that it involved, so that He could say, "The Father is greater than I." This willingness was put into practice, so that

2. He emptied Himself. He laid aside His divine form and His rights as God. He had a reputation, but He made Himself of no reputation. He gave up His position as God and His being as God and accepted to come down to this earth, leaving aside the glory of heaven. Had He not been humble, He would have said, "Father I accept the second place to You, but let me go to earth with the glory of heaven. Let me perhaps go as an archangel. Let me be different in form from these people." He did not think or act that way. Rather,

3. He was made in the likeness of men. He put aside His divine being and took upon Himself our humanity with its limitations, so much so that He was limited by space and time; He could become hungry, tired and weary. He became truly man!

4. He took the form of a slave. The Lord did not say, "I will become man, but I must become an important man, a king or a president." So He became not an important man, but a servant and a slave. He became a man in the

lowest grade of men - a slave; one who had no right whatsoever.

5. He did not become an important slave but the lowliest of slaves - the one on whom men spat. He became a suffering slave, a Man of sorrows and one from whom men hid their faces.

6. Even as a lowly slave, the Lord Jesus humbled Himself further. He became a slave who was doomed not to live but to die. He lived for thirty-three years with the knowledge of a death sentence upon Him, yet He was not discouraged or put off by that. He lived and enjoyed life to the fullest, even though He knew he would die 'young.'

7. Even as a slave doomed to die He humbled Himself still further. He could have said, "l will die, but let Me die respectably. l do not want further shame." He did not say that. He accepted the most humbling death - death on a cross. He died, not like a righteous man or like an ordinary man. He died like a criminal, the worst class of criminals, for only such were crucified. He died as a curse, for it was said, "Cursed is everyone who hangs on a tree." He went to the lowest level of degradation. He hit rock-bottom. By giving Himself for death on the cross, the Lord Jesus reached the very depth of humiliation. He was the very embodiment of humility. No one can ever become more humble than He did. Can you imagine the difference between what He was by right and the point to which, by voluntary choice, He brought Himself? No one will ever start from the height from which He started, and few will ever reach the depths of self-abasement that He reached. He is the supreme example.

The Lord did not remain in the depths of humiliation for ever. God raised Him and exalted Him. God raised Him from the depths of self-abasement to the highest height. He also did this in seven steps of exaltation.

1. God exalted Him. This is wonderful; for it is God who exalted Him. Men can give honours, offices and respect. They appoint to a high position and have you receive much praise, but the day you are removed from office, all that glory departs and you are despised. While Chairman Mao Tse Tung of China was alive, people came close to worshipping him and his word was law. When he died, the same people who had worshipped him exposed his weaknesses and crimes. They could have tried and condemned him. The honour was all gone. Men did not exalt Jesus. The Father did. That honour and exaltation can never be taken away from Him. Sometimes men praise and confer honours without knowing the truth about the person they are honouring, and if they knew the whole truth, they would change their minds completely. God, however, knew all of Christ and God appointed Him to exaltation.

2. God did not only exalt Him, but God highly exalted Him. God exalted Him to the highest height. The position to which Jesus is exalted is the highest in heaven. The highest, most exalted throne in heaven is His. Yes, Jesus was highly exalted with all the honour and glory of heaven.

3. God bestowed upon Him a name. He was not exalted to the very heights and left without a name. He was given a name that is above every other name. I want to say that God raised the name of Jesus even above His own name.

That being true, we can then think of all the lesser names: Name the name of the greatest

President,

King,

Scientist,

Inventor,

 etc,

and you know that the name of Jesus is greater. He humbled Himself below all names in order that He might receive a name that surpasses all the others.

4. The glorious name of Jesus is one to which people must bow. In heaven all the glorious beings fall down and worship Him. Even the twenty-four elders, who are perhaps the highest created order in heaven, fall down before Him and sing a new song, saying, *"Worthy art thou to take the scroll and to open its seals, for thou wast slain and by thy blood didst ransom men for God from every tribe and tongue and people and nation, and hast made them a kingdom and priests to our God, and they shall reign on earth"* (Revelation 5:9-10). In heaven, therefore, angels, archangels, seraphim, cherubim, etc, bow at His name.

5. On earth where His authority is questioned, we are told that all knees shall bow at His name. All the knees of all human beings who have ever lived on earth, who are living on earth and who will ever live on earth, must bow to the Lord Jesus. The obedient bow now and the disobedient wait to bow from the lake of fire. It does not matter the place from which they bow, but all must bow.

You shall bow. Will you bow now and be right with Him or will you bow then from despair?

6. All knees under the earth shall also bow. The glory of Jesus, as we see, shall be fully recognized in heaven. There is no problem there even now. It shall also be recognized by the bowing of knees on earth. The Lord will have His authority and glory recognized by <u>all</u> human beings, regardless of whether or not they want to. To crown it all, at the name of Jesus all the knees of all the beings under the earth shall bow. Those under the earth are those of the kingdom of the wicked one. Satan shall bow and all his principalities, powers, thrones, rulers of the darkness of this world, demons, etc, shall bow to Him. This is really great; for by being humble, He became the One before whom the greatest forces of the enemy shall bow.

7. It would have been easier to bow and keep quiet, but the name that Jesus has been given is so great that in heaven and on earth and under the earth, all who bow shall confess that Jesus is Lord and, to seal it all up, this confession shall bring total satisfaction to the Father.

Jesus was thus exalted; but He had first humbled Himself. Jesus humbled Himself and God raised Him up. If it had become necessary for God to humble Him because of His pride, there would have been no one to exalt Him. We say, then that:

God exalts those who humble themselves. God humbles those who exalt themselves and there is no one then to exalt them.

1.   The call to humility

The Lord Jesus did not only set a supreme example of humility, but He invites people to it. He said, *"Come to me, all who labour and are heavy laden, and I will give you rest. Take my yoke upon you, and learn from me; for I am gentle and lowly in heart, and you will find rest for your souls"* (Matthew 11:28-29).

James said, *"God opposes the proud, but gives grace to the humble. Submit yourselves therefore to God"* (James 4:6-7).

The apostle Peter said, *"Clothe yourselves, all of you, with humility towards one another, for 'God opposes the proud, but gives grace to the humble.' Humble yourselves therefore under the mighty hand of God, that in due time he may exalt you"* (1 Peter 5:5-6).

2.   What is humility, meekness, lowliness?

Humility is the state of mind in which a person does <u>nothing</u> from selfishness or conceit. He does nothing to cause people to think of him more highly than he is. He does nothing to give a more elevated picture of himself. Humility is the state of mind in which a person submits totally to the sovereignty of God and never dares question anything that God has done. Humility is a state of mind in which a person counts others better than himself. Humility is the state of mind in which a person looks not only to his own interests, but to the interests of others; where others are put first.

Meekness is the state of mind in which a person who has great power and great abilities holds these in check. Instead of displaying them in order to draw attention to himself or to establish his importance, he puts all his great power and abilities at the service of God and other human beings without counting what it is costing him. Meekness is not the state of mind where a person who can do nothing just sits down and does nothing. To be meek, a person must have much and yet hold it in check. For example, the Lord Jesus said that He was meek. His meekness was manifested not by the absence of great power and ability, but by the refusal to use these for self-display or for selfish interests. He could have called legions of angels to His aid, but He did not.

Lowliness is the state of mind in which a person deliberately and constantly chooses the way that exalts Christ and the others, instead of the way that exalts himself. Lowliness is a state of mind that is entered into by choice, and not something forced upon a person. The lowly person knows that he could exalt himself, but he decides not to do it and rather abases himself, and does it without any feeling of condescension.

When this state of mind is entered into and maintained, then the person is humble, meek and lowly.

3.   Humility (how acquired)

There is a sense in which humility is not something that can be learnt. It is not something that can be acquired by saying, "Let me take this lowly seat this time, let me not show off," etc. Humility is acquired by revelation.

When God opens a person's eyes to see the Lord Jesus in all His wondrous beauty and glory, that person will for ever be humble before Him. When a person's eyes are opened to see the greatness, power, etc, of the God of heaven, that person will be humble before Him and will acknowledge that such a

God can only do that which is right. He will, from that moment on, worship the Lord and never question Him.

When a person's eyes are opened to see himself as he is outside the grace of God - sinful, rotten, bankrupt, powerless, etc, he will cease to have inflated and false opinions about himself. When his eyes are opened to see the fact that, but for the restraining grace of God, he could commit the worst sin possible and that he is able to commit any and all sins, he will not consider himself anything great. He will forever remain prostrate before God and cry out like the tax collector, *"God, be merciful to me a sinner"* (Luke 18:13). When a person's eyes are opened to the fact that what he knows of the failures of another person is only part of the story; that God knows the reasons, motivations, temptations, trials and victories of the person, about which he knows nothing, he will cease to judge others and stop comparing them negatively with himself. When a person's eyes are opened to the fact that there is nothing that he has either of natural endowments or of spiritual gifts that he did not receive, he will forever be humble; for the One who gave can take them away and the One who gives can give even more to the despised person. When a person's eyes are opened to the dangers of a life that is not humble, meek and lowly, that person will at once cry to the Lord Jesus and say to Him, "Lord Jesus, make me humble."

The problem with too many believers is that they have only a mental grasp of these things. They know them only intellectually. They have not had them revealed to them and, therefore, they do not "see." They can, therefore, recite these truths and yet remain untouched, with the reality totally absent in their lives. Realizing their need for revelation, the apostle Paul prayed for the believers at Ephesus that, *"The Father of glory, may give you a spirit of wisdom and of revelation in the knowledge of him, having the eyes of your hearts enlightened, that you may know what is the hope to which he has called you, what are the riches of his glorious inheritance in the saints"* (Ephesians 1:17-18).

When a person sees with the natural mind, he can remain proud. When he sees with the eyes of the heart that have been enlightened, he cannot be the same. He will be humble.

When a person has been enabled by the Lord to see God, himself and other people as God sees them, his entire attitude will be different. He has encountered a major crisis. He will in each situation immediately see pride for what it is and also see the blessedness of humility. If he should continue to walk with God in obedience to the leading of the Holy Spirit, that which was imparted of humility to him when God opened his eyes and he "saw" for the first time, will be fully worked out by the Holy Spirit in his life until the humility of Christ is fully established in him.

This further working out of humility is often carried out by the Holy Spirit with the use of the Cross:

1. The Holy Spirit will reveal any traces of abiding inhumility or any attempts to develop inhumility and show these up as sin to be confessed and forsaken.

2. The Holy Spirit will lead the person to situations where any traces of pride are exposed through failure until the person's confidence in himself is destroyed completely.

3. The Holy Spirit will continue to reveal Jesus Christ in an ever-increasing way until the student in the "School of Humility" is caught up with Christ and with Him alone, and there remains no place for the self in him to exhibit itself.

When this has been worked out in a life, the person's reactions will change completely. For example, in the past when someone spoke something evil of him, he would do one of three things:

1. Speak something bad of that person.
2. Reply back and explain with the desire to change the picture so painted of him.
3. Keep quiet but boil inside with resentment.

The person who has made progress in the School of Humility has been liberated from the opinion of men. When someone says something negative of him, he will not take any offence whatsoever. He will not feel bad inside. He will not defend himself at all. He will acknowledge that he is actually worse than the person has said that he is, even if the area that the person has picked out may lack accuracy. He may even tell the person, "1 am worse than that but, by grace, 1 have been accepted." By so acting, he dies more and more to self and becomes more and more alive to Christ.

A person in whom God has worked out this humility will never give up any one. He will see the possibility of God changing even the worst person alive and will co-operate with God so that that change takes place.

The humble person will never say, "1 cannot commit that kind of sin." He knows that, but for the grace of God, he would commit sins that are more terrible. He will never trust in himself. He has taken the injunction of the writer of Proverbs which says, *"Trust in the Lord with all your heart, and do not rely on your own insight. In all your ways acknowledge him, and he will make straight your path"* (Proverbs 3:5-6).

The humble person is glad when others are praised and he is not disturbed when they are compared more favourably with him. He is at peace. He has nothing to protect. He has abandoned all unreservedly on the Lord Jesus and been liberated from the praises of the world.

The humble person gives himself to the service of others. He puts the others first in everything. If there is praise, he gives it first to others.

If there is some gain, he lets others have it first.

If there is labour, he gives himself to it first.

If there is suffering, he takes the first place.

By constantly giving himself away to others, and by constantly giving the best places to others, he takes the last one, not because he could not take the first place, but because he counted others worthy of greater honour than himself. He is not inferior. He is not plagued with fear and failure, since he has known the liberating power of God's grace. He is at the bottom because he put some others on the top.

A humble person will never say, "This job is below my dignity." He is a disciple of the Lord Jesus who *"rose from supper, laid aside his garments, and girded himself with a towel. Then he poured water into a basin, and began to wash the disciples' feet, and to wipe them with the towel with which he was girded"* (John 13:4-5). He does all the jobs that need to be done and he goes in particularly for those jobs that those who are ignorant would not do. He is a servant.

4.   The dangers of inhumility (pride)

Those who are not humble are proud. If a person would not put on humility, he would put on pride or leave pride on. What are the dangers of pride? What is the lot of those who do not learn humility from the Lord Jesus? We shall outline just a few of the many dangers that befall the proud.

1. They are opposed by God. The Bible says, *"God opposes the proud"* (James 4:6).

2. They are an abomination to the Lord. The Bible says, *"Every one who is arrogant is an abomination to the Lord; be assured, he will not go unpunished"* (Proverbs 16:5).

3. They are hated by the Lord. *"Pride and arrogance and the way of evil and perverted speech I hate"* (Proverbs 8:13).

4. They are disgraced. *"When pride comes, then comes disgrace"* (Proverbs 11:2).

5. Their dwelling is torn down by the Lord. *"The Lord tears down the house of the proud"* (Proverbs 15:25).

6. They end in destruction. *"Pride goes before destruction, and a haughty spirit before a fall"* (Proverbs 16:18).

Pride originated from the devil. Of him, the Bible says, *"How you are fallen from heaven, O Day Star, son of Dawn! How you are cut down to the ground, you who laid the nations low! You said in your heart, 'I will ascend to heaven; above the stars of God, I will set my throne on high; I will sit on the mount of assembly in the far north. I will ascend above the heights of the clouds, I will make myself like the Most High.' But you are brought down to Sheol, to the depths of the pit. Those who see you will stare at you, and ponder over you: Is this the man who made the earth tremble, who shook kingdoms, who made the world a desert and overthrew its cities?"* (Isaiah 14:12-17) Satan fell because of pride. All who are proud will fall as he did. The characteristic of Lucifer that led to his fall was that his life was centered around "l."

He said,   "l will ascend to heaven."

"l will set my throne."

"l will sit on the mount."

"l will ascend above the heights."

"l will make myself like the Most High."

Another person, Nebuchadnezzar, thought and spoke like him and was punished for his pride. He said, *"Is not this great Babylon, which I have built by my mighty power as a royal residence and for the glory of my majesty?' While the words were still in the King's mouth, there fell a voice from heaven. 'O king Nebuchadnezzar, to you is spoken: The kingdom has departed from you, and you shall be driven from among men, and your dwelling shall be with the beasts of the field; and you shall be made to eat grass like an ox; and seven times shall pass over you, until you have learned that the Most High rules the kingdom of men and gives it to whom he wills"* (Daniel 4:30-32).

The proud of heart cannot fellowship with the Lord Jesus, since He is meek and lowly of heart. They can neither know the fullness of the Holy Spirit nor the fullness of God's power, since the Holy Spirit can only fill those who have come to the end of themselves - those who are humble.

Pride keeps people away from entering by the narrow gate; and if they do enter, the log of pride limits them very severely. The more the pride, the more the world and the more the devil.

5. The blessings of humility, meekness, lowliness

1. *"The meek and lowly will have fellowship with the Lord Jesus"* (Matthew 11:29-30).

2. The humble receive grace from the Lord. *"God..... gives grace to the humble"* (James 4:6).

3. The humble are exalted by the Lord. *"Humble yourselves before the Lord and he will exalt you"* (James 4:10).

4. The humble possess wisdom. *"With the humble is wisdom"* (Proverbs 11:2).

5. The humble will receive honour. *"Humility goes before honour"* (Proverbs 15:33).

6. The humble experience God's deliverance. *"Thou dost deliver a humble people"* (2 Samuel 22:28).

7. They receive guidance from the Lord. *"He leads the humble in what is right, and teaches the humble his way"* (Psalm 25:9).

8. The humble are granted victory by the Lord. *"For the Lord takes pleasure in his people; he adorns the humble with victory"* (Psalm 149:4).

9. The humble are God's dwelling-place and He revives their spirit. *"For thus says the high and lofty One who inhabits eternity, whose name is Holy: 'I dwell in the high and holy place, and also with him who is of a contrite and humble spirit, to revive the spirit of the humble, and to revive the heart of the contrite'"* (Isaiah 57:15).

10. The meek inherit the earth. *"Blessed are the meek, for they shall inherit the earth"* (Matthew 5:5).

11. The meek shall obtain fresh joy in the Lord. *"The meek shall obtain fresh joy in the Lord, and the poor among men shall exult in the Holy one of Israel"* (Isaiah 29:19).

12. The lowly are set to rule. *"The Most High rules the kingdom of men"* (Daniel 4:17).

In addition, the humble are saved from many errors because they are more open to correction. They are also in better health than the proud who suffer each time something happens that deflates their pride. They walk close to the Lord, since He does not resist them.

6. Some practical issues

We said that humility is the product of a threefold revelation of the greatness of God, the weakness of man and the folly of pride. Someone may then say, "Should l then continue as l am until the day when my heart's eyes are opened to these things? Is there nothing that l can begin to do to co-operate with God so that my pride is dealt with and l am rendered humble?" l think that there are things that you should start doing while waiting for further light.

I want to say that because you know, even if it is only intellectually, that humility is God's will for you and that pride is of the wicked one and, therefore, sinful, you are responsible for that knowledge. Act upon it and then God will give you further light.

1. Begin to listen more to others and talk less. Try not to dominate conversations. Give more room to others.

2. Begin to talk less about yourself:

   − what you are and what you have.

   − what you have done.

   − what you intend to do.

1. Begin to keep some of your accomplishments and experiences to yourself. If you have done something really good, keep quiet about it. If you have had a fresh touch from the Lord, do not tell anyone about it. Let people see its effects on your life.

2. Begin to talk more about the accomplishments of others, especially those of people whom you would rather drag down. When someone does something very bad, think about something that is good about the person and, instead of exposing his faults to others, expose that which is good about him. Decide that you will not speak evil of anyone nor ever say anything in a person's absence which will hurt his reputation. Never compare anyone to yourself to your advantage.

3. Begin to expose some of your faults and failures and help people to have a true picture of what you are. Be a hypocrite no more.

4. Begin to look for opportunities to serve others instead of waiting to be served. If you get to a place where practical work is being done, or some other work in which you could help, join in at once and do not wait to be invited. Offer to serve at table, clean dishes and the floor. Begin to give the first place to others in entering buses, trains, etc. Do not push your way ahead of the others. Do not defend your rights. If need be, allow yourself to be down-trodden. God will exalt you when you are low enough.

5. Ask the Lord to lead you in the way that will bring you into contact with experiences and people who will humble you.

6. Do not go for the places of honour at parties, meetings, etc.

7. Confess every act of arrogance, conceit and pride. These are dangerous sins. Confess and forsake them.

8. Thank the Lord for every manifestation of the humility of the Lord Jesus in you.

7.   Finally, does it matter to you?

Many believers will agree without much hesitation that they are proud and far from humble. This is good. The thing that causes worry is that they should be content, after such a confession, to go on without doing anything about it.

The sin of pride has been accepted as part of the life of believers.

If a believer stole, would you be comfortable about it? I think not.

If he killed, wouldn't you be shocked? I believe you would.

If he made a graven image, you might at once pass him for an unbeliever.

These are serious sins and all sins are serious.

What of pride? Who was ever denied fellowship because he was proud? Who was ever asked not to break bread because he was proud? Yet, which is more grievous, pride or theft? A man may be tempted to steal and he may fall into the sin of stealing once, then repent and be forgiven, but what of pride? Because pride is a permanent sin, permanent until it is radically dealt with, the proud of heart are living in perpetual sin. Yet their sin is at the root of all sins. Pride is the greatest sin.

How sad it is to know that people claim to be filled with the Holy Spirit and the same people are filled with pride! Filled with the Holy Spirit (the Spirit of humility, meekness and lowliness) and filled with pride (the spirit of conceit, arrogance, self-exaltation)? It does not take much effort to see that the proud of heart are not filled with the Holy Spirit. We know that God resists the proud. How can He resist them and then fill them at the same time? How can He fill the proud, whom He hates, while they continue in their pride? The impossibility of this is obvious for all who want to see. So when proud, arrogant self-advertisers claim to be filled with the Holy Spirit, they are hypocrites who, by their false claim, make it more difficult for the Spirit of God to help them.

Now, what about you? Are you proud or humble? If you are proud, do not rest until God has done a deep and radical work in you to make you humble. Co-operate with God by humbling yourself. If you are sincere and determined, God will act quickly and deeply.

If you are humble, praise the Lord for it. Keep alert so that the devil may not drag you into pride. Ask the Lord to take you into deeper experiences in the "School of Humility" and how blessed you shall be! God bless you!   Glory be to the Lord!

"If anyone would be first, he must be last of all and servant of all" (Mark 9:35).   *"Whoever humbles himself like this child, he is the greatest in the kingdom of heaven"* (Matthew 18:4).

Discipline (self-control)

Discipline is the spiritual art of putting soul and body under control, so that they obey the dictates of the Spirit spontaneously.

1. GOD DISCIPLINES

The Lord Jesus said, *"I am the true vine, and my Father is the vinedresser. Every branch of mine that bears no fruit, he takes away, and every branch that does bear fruit he prunes, that it may bear more fruit"* (John 15:1-2). The pruning so that it may bear more fruit is disciplining. The Bible further says, *"My son, do not despise the Lord's discipline or be weary of his reproof, for the Lord reproves him whom he loves, as a father the son in whom he delights"* (Proverbs 3:11-12). The Bible says, *"Consider him who endured from sinners such hostility against himself, so that you may not grow weary or faint-hearted. In your struggle against sin you have not yet resisted to the point of shedding your blood. And have you forgotten the exhortation which addresses you as sons? 'My son, do not regard lightly the discipline of the Lord, nor lose courage when you are punished by him: For the Lord disciplines him whom he loves, and chastises every son whom he receives.' It is for discipline that you have to endure. God is treating you as sons; for what son is there whom his father does not discipline? If you are left without discipline, in which all have participated, then you are illegitimate children and not sons. Besides this, we have had earthly fathers to discipline us and we respected them. Shall we not much more be subject to the Father of spirits and live? For they disciplined us for a short time at their pleasure, but he disciplines us for our good, that we may share his holiness. For the moment all discipline seems painful rather than pleasant; later it yields the peaceful fruit of righteousness to those who have been trained by it. Therefore lift your drooping hands and strengthen your weak knees, and make straight paths for your feet, so that what is lame may not be put out of joint but rather be healed. Strive for peace with all men, and for the holiness without which no one will see the Lord. See to it that no one fail to obtain the grace of God"* (Hebrews 12:3-15).

God's purpose for disciplining His children is that they may share His holiness; that His children should have the peaceful fruit of righteousness produced in them. So discipline is not an end. It is the means to an end - the holiness of God imparted to His children.

The Christian's purpose for discipline must be the same with God's - holiness, righteousness, the accomplishment of God's will. This distinguishes Christian discipline from worldly discipline. Worldly discipline has as the goal the acquisition of some earthly honor in sports, academics, etc.

God disciplines His children by many ways. For example, He beats them into shape by the use of His Word, by the circumstances of life, etc. No believer should take over the work of God in disciplining in that way. However, the believer is called to co-operate with God by disciplining himself. That which the believer must do in his self-discipline will never be done by God and that believer will fail who leaves to God what he must do.

The apostle Paul was concerned that there be discipline and he himself was committed to discipline. He said, *"Every athlete exercises self-control in all things. They do it to receive a perishable wreath, but we an imperishable. Well, I do not run aimlessly, I do not box as one beating the air, but I pommel my body and subdue it, lest after preaching to others I myself should be disqualified"* (1 Corinthians 9:25-27).

In athletics we have a goal - a prize to be won. In order that that prize is won, the athlete exercises self-control (discipline) in <u>ALL</u> things. He exercises self-control in his speech, food, practice, drinking habits, etc. In fact, he exercises self-control in everything that will directly or indirectly affect his performance in the race. He wants to do everything possible in order to win.

The apostle Paul said that the crown that the athlete was aiming at was a perishable one, yet he put everything into winning it.

The believer also has a crown to win the crown of life which Jesus the righteous Judge will give him on that day, yet not only to him, but also to all who love His appearing.

With that in view, the apostle had a clear aim. He did not run aimlessly. He ran with that goal (the crown of life) in view. He did not beat the air. He only did those things that would help him to win the crown. All other good things were useless, so long as they did not help him to win the crown of life. He, therefore, did not do any such good but useless things. He judged, assessed, and evaluated everything, every idea, every person, as that one related to the goal in view. He did not ask what would make him happy. That was not important. He asked what would help him to win the crown of life.

In order to win the crown, not only did he not run aimlessly or waste his blows, but he pommeled his body and subdued it so that his body, instead of being an obstacle, became a servant in helping him to win the crown of life.

We shall limit ourselves in the rest of this message to this matter of not wasting blows and of subduing the body.

2. THE CHRISTIAN'S DISCIPLINE

We must state clearly what the Christian's goal is. It is to win Christ and to be all that Christ saved him for and wants him to be. This involves character and service. The question before us then is, "How can a believer discipline himself, bring his body under control, not waste his blows, so that he will be what Christ saved him for and wants him to be?"

We readily acknowledge that only the disciplined Christian will go very far with God. All the others who also believe in the Lord Jesus but are not disciplined, will not go as far as the disciplined.

We shall look at different areas needing discipline and comment freely on these as the Lord leads us.

3. PURPOSE

Many people have no over-riding purpose for their lives. Such have already failed. How can anyone win a crown that he does not know to exist? How can an athlete win who does not know to what point he is running? So the first thing to be done in the School of Discipline is to receive from the Lord that which He has called you to do for Him. Without this, much of life would be confused activity. It would be misguided zeal. So many people say, "My purpose in life is to serve the Lord and to serve only Him." That is good religious language. We ask, "How has the Lord asked you to serve Him?" Without this clear knowledge, you could waste your life doing some religious or Christian work to which He did not call you. There are some who believe that they are to serve the Lord by doing everything. There are members of the body who think that, instead of being members, they should individually become the body. This cannot work. Anyone who is interested in too many things will fail in life. Such a person will jump from one area of service to the other. He will be moved by need. Every rising need will cause him to jump and offer some help. His energies will then be dispersed, and his accomplishments superficial.

Paul said, "This one thing I do." The disciplined person has only one area of specialization. It is that which the Lord has given him to do for Him. He sticks to that and does it for the Lord. He leaves aside many other good things which could be done for the Lord and the Church, but to which the Lord has not called him as an individual.

This requires a lot of discipline. If he has many abilities, he will be able to do many things very well. If he is very gifted, he may be able to minister in many areas. However, the question is not, "Where can I minister with a fair measure of success?" but "What has the Lord called me to do for Him?"

Discipline means that the person will not allow himself to be moved by any of the following:

1. The needs of the Church(es)
2. The shortage of workers

3. The good that could result from his effort

4. The insistence of the brethren, etc.

Many good, spiritual things will present themselves, but he will say, "No," to them. Sometimes it will pierce his heart to say, "No," but he will do it. The brethren may not understand, but he must say, "No." Trying circumstances, false brethren, backsliders, and the like may tempt him, but he will refuse to yield to any such temptation. He will just stick to that which God has asked him to do and leave the rest to the Lord.

If laborer's are few, he will not jump from here to there in order to do the work of others because these others are

1. not available

2. immature

3. lazy

4. discouraged, etc.

He will not leave that which the Lord has called him to do, or add to that which the Lord has called him do in order to increase understanding and harmony among the brethren. By adding to that which the Lord gave him to do, he has stepped into the place from which he will cause confusion, for the only way not to cause confusion is to stay within God's specific call.

All God's children must abide in that to which the Lord has called them. That call by the Lord is meant to occupy every second of their lives until they go to be with the Lord. There is no possibility of adding to it and yet accomplishing it. All who add the work of others to theirs will fail to complete theirs. All God's children must receive from the Lord and abide absolutely in what the Lord has called them. This is the only way to satisfy the Lord. Anything else is utter failure. To move from the realm of the call of God to any other realm, because that realm has fewer problems and promises more success, is to fail utterly.

When a person has disciplined himself with regard to his purpose, he must then work at the following areas to ensure that his goal is achieved.

4. THE DISCIPLINE OF THE SPIRIT

The believer is meant, by the Lord, to be controlled by his spirit. It is God's purpose that the spirit should control the soul which should in turn control the body.

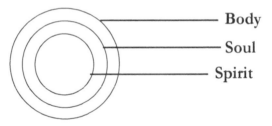

God meant that the spirit of man would control his soul, which would in turn control his body.

At conversion everyone has his spirit made alive by the Holy Spirit who comes to dwell in the spirit of man. The human spirit is controlled either by the Holy Spirit or by the soul. The person who habitually yields to the Holy Spirit will have his spirit develop the right authority and so govern the soul which, in turn, governs the body. The spirit can, on the other hand, be governed by the soul. If the soul receives information, it will influence the spirit and, depending on what the information is, the spirit will react accordingly. So, what happens in the spirit will affect the soul, and the type of information that the soul receives will influence the spirit. So your spirit can be in different conditions:

1. *"Why does your heart carry you away, and do your eyes flash, that you turn your spirit against God, and let such words go out of your mouth?"* (Job 15:12-13).

2. *"Blessed is the man to whom the Lord imputes no iniquity, and in whose spirit there is no deceit"* (Psalm 32:2).

3. *"The Lord is near to the brokenhearted, and saves the crushed in spirit"* (Psalm 34:18).

4. *".....A generation whose heart was not steadfast, whose spirit was not faithful to God"* (Psalm 78:8).

5. *"And it went ill with Moses on their account; for they made his spirit bitter, and he spoke words that were rash"* (Psalm 106:32-33).

6. *"When my spirit is faint, thou knowest my way"* (Psalm 142:3).

7. *"The Lord weighs the spirit"* (Proverbs 16:2).

8. *"A cheerful heart is a good medicine, but a downcast spirit dries up the bones"* (Proverbs 17:22).

9. *"A man's spirit will endure sickness; but a broken spirit who can bear?"* (Proverbs 18:14).

10. *"The spirit of man is the lamp of the Lord, searching all his innermost parts"* (Proverbs 20:27).

11. *"Blessed are the poor in spirit, for theirs is the kingdom of heaven"* (Matthew 5:3).

By constant obedience to the Holy Spirit and by feeding on the Word, etc, man co-operates with the Holy Spirit to render his spirit normal. Furthermore, by controlling what happens in his soul, man also controls the type of information that comes to bear on the spirit and, in this way, either helps to render the spirit normal or abnormal. A normal spirit is that which has the soul totally under control, it itself being totally obedient to the Holy Spirit.

We shall not discuss the control of the spirit any further except to insist that the following verses of Scripture be taken seriously.

1. *"If you set your heart aright, you will stretch out your hands toward him"* (Job 11:13).
2. *"Keep your heart with all vigilance; for from it flow the springs of life"* (Proverbs 4:23).
3. *"Blessed are the pure in heart, for they shall see God".* (Matthew 5:8).

(The heart is a part of the human spirit.)

5. THE DISCIPLINE OF THE SOUL

The human soul is made up of the mind (for thinking), the will (for deciding) and the emotions (for feeling). All these three must be brought under discipline. They could be considered separately, but we shall look at factors that often involve all of them together.

1. Thoughts

The Bible says, *"The thoughts of the righteous are just"* (Proverbs 12:5). However, the righteous must continue to be righteous for his thoughts to continue to be just. The thoughts can become impure and sinful or they can be rendered pure and holy. The crucial thing then will be what the person allows to come into his mind.

A disciplined person will ensure that he controls what enters into his thoughts and that he controls what his mind concentrates on. To have a mind that wanders all over this country, then all over the continent, is a mark of tragic indiscipline. Having a mind that cannot concentrate in prayer, Bible study, etc, is a sin of an undisciplined person. Thoughts that are allowed to wander at will may land on sin and soon begin to feast upon it, and the undisciplined person may not recognize the fact that things are going wrong until his thoughts have led him into tragic action.

Because sins committed in thoughts are equally grievous before the Lord, the need to have thoughts under control becomes very serious. We suggest the following process in achieving discipline in your thoughts:

1. Confess all known sins committed in your life and forsake them.

2. Acknowledge the fact that your thoughts have been undisciplined.

3. Confess this sin of indiscipline to the Lord and ask Him to forgive you.

4. Ask the Holy Spirit to fill your life completely.

5. Set your being on thinking one thing at a time. If you are thinking about your studies, refuse any other thought that comes into your mind to distract you. You will find that the distracting thought is that of something less serious and probably vain or sinful. Labour to keep your thoughts on the object of thought until you have completely finished with that subject. If some thought

comes to you, reject it and get back to your subject of concentration.

6. Do not allow your mind to go blank. Fill it with positive and good thoughts, so that there will be no room for the sinful thoughts. The Bible says, *"Whatever is true, whatever is honourable, whatever is just, whatever is pure, whatever is lovely, whatever is gracious, if there is any excellence, if there is anything worthy of praise, think about these things"* (Philippians 4:8).

7. Do not run away from hard, clear thinking. If you just drift in your thoughts, you will continue in indiscipline.

8. Use aids like jotting down the subjects you are, say, praying about.

9. Be totally taken up with what the Lord has called you to do for Him. The thoughts of that thing will soon fill you so much so that when you are not actively thinking, your mind will come to rest on the Lord and on that thing. This is good resting ground for your thought life.

10. If you have problems with impure (sexual thoughts), make sure that there are no objects like suggestive pictures or books around to arouse twisted thoughts. If you meet a beautiful girl, pray for her in this way: "Lord, I thank You for this beautiful girl. Help her so that her beauty may not lead her to sin, and grant me grace not to lust after her beauty in my heart."

11. If you have a sudden thought that your enemy ought to die or something evil should happen to him, these are the fiery darts of the devil. Command such wicked thoughts to go away from you at once.

12. Fill your mind with the Word of the Lord. The Psalmist says, *"How can a young man keep his way pure? By guarding*

it according to thy word. With my whole heart I seek thee; let me not wander from thy commandments! I have laid up thy word in my heart, that I might not sin against thee" (Psalm 119:9-11).

2. Discipline of the physical body

The physical body is not an enemy to righteousness. Rather, it is a servant to be tamed and then used. To a very large extent, a person can control the following things about his body:

1. The shape of his body - whether he is smart or clumsy will depend on him.

2. Size - whether he is slim and handsome or fat and clumsy will depend on him.

3. Weight - whether he is normal weight or overweight will, to a large extent, be determined by him. If he eats without discipline, he will possibly be over-weight. Almost all overweight people commit the sin of gluttony. There are, however, other gluttons who do not show this in their body size.

4. Muscles - whether a person's muscles are strong or flabby will largely depend on whether or not he exercises his body.

5. Teeth - whether or not his teeth are clean depends not on God but on him.

The believer who is bent on pleasing the Lord Jesus will discipline his body. He will control:

a. what he eats

b. when he eats

c. what quantities he eats

d. how he eats.

He will not eat what will prevent him from building the strongest physical body with which to serve the Lord. His motto will be: "Everything that enters into my mouth must be such that helps me to be the best soldier that l can be for the glory of the Lord Jesus. l will ensure that everything l eat gives me the best looks that will say, 'This is what Jesus is like.'"

With that goal in view, he will ask himself about every food placed before him, "Will eating this food help me to be like Jesus and to look like Jesus?" If eating anything will create a bad impression of the Master he represents, he will say, "No." When he has eaten enough, he must say, "No," to any invitation from inside or outside to have a second helping. He must not pack excess weight on his body in order to please someone who would be offended if he did not eat. He must not commit the sin of gluttony to please anyone. How can he afford to displease God and please man? If he is overweight, he must immediately do something about it. When a man is ten or fifteen kilos overweight and condemns the person who commits the sin of immorality once, I wonder who is more to be blamed - the overweight man who commits the sin of indiscipline over food as a way of life or the person who committed one act of indiscipline over his sexual urge?

When a Christian has decided to fast, begins the fast and somewhere along the line gives up the fast because of a temptation to eat, that one is a fool who put his hands to the plough but looked back. God takes no pleasure in such fools. Hunger is largely a feeling. It will not kill. Infact, the feeling will go away when resisted.

No believer should just eat anything, anywhere and at any time. He must be conscious of what he is doing. He should eat with thanksgiving. He must seek God's approval for all that he wants to put into the temple of God, which is his body.

All who want to represent the Lord must dress in a disciplined way. Their clothes must be clean and presentable. Their bodies must be washed and they must look serious and responsible. That believer whose teeth are not brushed, whose body has a strong body odour because of no care and whose clothes single him out as a beggar, is unlikely to be taken seriously by anyone. Many people are likely to think that whatever he has to offer cannot be more serious than his looks say he is. Some unbeliever said, "By my looks and my dressing, l must preach my gospel." Should a believer develop a philosophy that demands less than that from him?

We know that the body can be trained to serve in any direction. If it is trained to need two meals a day, it will find that sufficient; and if it is trained to need five meals a day, it will complain when it is given only four meals any day. If it is trained to accept dirt, you can go without bathing for days, but if it is trained to be clean, it will react if a bath has not been taken for twenty-four hours.

The choice is yours, then, as to what you make your body into. If you want your body to best represent the Lord and serve the interest of the Kingdom, you will pommel it and subdue it, and so transform it into a servant. The beginning of the process will be unpleasant, but at the end it will be a useful servant to help you to accomplish great things for God. Will you do something about it?

3.   Disciplined use of time

Although God has given different spiritual gifts to His children and different talents to His created beings, He has given everyone the same amount of time. All human beings have each been given twenty-four hours each day.

The sad thing is the differences in the accomplishments of people, depending upon their use of the time that God has given them. Some people use the time that God has given them while others waste it.

For time to be properly used, life's goal must be had and life's priorities sorted out and discipline applied to ensure that what must be done is done and what must be done first is done first.

Disciplined use of time means that a person writes down: "The purpose of my life is X. Anything that contributes to accomplish X will be done. Anything that does not contribute towards the accomplishment of X will not be done." So, for such a person, there are no neutral things. Everything that helps him is positive and every other thing is negative because, even if it lacks any inherent danger, it will nevertheless stand in the way of X by taking up precious time that ought to have been devoted to it. By doing so, it shows itself for what it actually is - an enemy under cover and, therefore, a greater enemy in a sense.

Having eliminated all that will not contribute to the accomplishment of X as bad and evil, the person who wants to glorify Christ will now come to that which gives the impression of contributing to the accomplishment of X and then ask, "Is there anything that only gives the impression of contributing towards the accomplishment of X but which actually does not?" On that basis a few things may again be eliminated.

After that, the serious person will ask, "Of these things that will help me to contribute to the accomplishment of X, which are the most important and which are the least important? On that basis he will make a list,

A. will contribute 10 points

B. will contribute 8 points

C. will contribute 6 points

D. will contribute 5 points

E. will contribute 4 points

F. will contribute 2 points

G. will contribute 1 point

H. will contribute 0.5 point

I. etc.

He will then make a priority list based on the impact of contribution as follows:

1. A

2. B

3. C

4. D

5. E

6. F

7. G

8. H, etc

From this priority list it becomes immediately obvious that even if it takes much time and a lot of effort to carry out the work labelled (a), its impact on the Kingdom will be greater than many (g's) and (h's). He will then ensure that if he hasn't the time to do all that can help him to accomplish his objective, he should concentrate on those that make the greatest impact. It needs discipline to stick to those things instead of running to the easier ones. There is a sense in which by concentrating on the things that contribute little, a person is beating the air and wasting his blows. He is running as if aimlessly. Anyone who would not pay the price of concentrating on the crucial things first will find that, by majoring on minors, he has misused his time and passed for a mediocre. l find the same thing happening among my students. Often the main questions which each carry twenty marks are left aside while the student concentrates on answering many questions that carry one or two marks. By doing this he jeopardizes his chances of passing; for the many questions that carry most of the marks are hurriedly attempted in the dying minutes of the examination. The wise student concentrates on the questions that carry the most marks, even if these are difficult, and attends to the ones that carry only a few marks each later on and, in this way, ensures that he obtains a good score.

Again we say, give your time first to the things that will contribute the most in helping you to accomplish your goal.

Another question that must be asked with regard to the use of time and the priorities of life is this: "What is there that will contribute significantly to the accomplishment of my goal which must be done at once because there will be no opportunity for its being done tomorrow?" If there are three things of real importance, the one which cannot wait without the opportunities for its being done being lost, must be done before the other things. There are things that must be done today, and if they are not done, the opportunity to do them will be lost for ever. Have you identified those things and are you concentrating on them? One of the things that cannot be stored is time. Every minute that is lost is lost for ever. A wasted day will never be recovered. Time is about the most perishable commodity that anyone can handle. Has that dawned on you and are you responding accordingly?

We make the following suggestions about discipline with regard to time:

1. Write out your goal clearly.

2. Write out the things that must be done to accomplish your goal.

3. Decide to concentrate only on the things written out in (2).

4. Distribute the things that must be done into years and months and days.

5. Write out today things that must be done tomorrow in the order of priority.

6. Refuse to push into tomorrow anything that must be done today. Determine that nothing will be postponed because it is unpleasant or difficult. Do the thing that you fear and see the death of fear.

7. Decide that you will not be lazy. Laziness is doing nothing with the time that God has given us. It is also doing too little with the time that is allotted to us or doing the wrong things and leaving the right things undone. Laziness is an abomination to the Lord. The Bible says, *"A son who gathers in summer is prudent, but a son who sleeps in harvest brings shame"* (Proverbs 10:5). *"Go to the ant, O sluggard; consider her ways, and be wise. Without having*

any chief, officer, or ruler, she prepares her food in summer, and gathers her sustenance in harvest. How long will you lie there, O sluggard? When will you arise from sleep? A little sleep, a little slumber, a little folding of the hands to rest, and poverty will come upon you like a vagabond, and want like an armed man" (Proverbs 6:6-11). The poverty could be spiritual poverty, for the undisciplined will end up being poor spiritually. The book of Proverbs describes a scene. l wonder if it is you who are being described. *"I passed by the field of a sluggard, by the vineyard of a man without sense; and lo, it was overgrown with thorns; the ground was covered with nettles, and its stone wall was broken down. Then I saw and considered it; I looked and received instruction. A little sleep, a little slumber, a little folding of the hands to rest, and poverty will come upon you like a robber, and want like an armed man"* (Proverbs 24:30-34).

The tragedy with indiscipline is that time is lost slowly, a little at a time. The sluggard did not say,

"l will sleep much,"

"l will slumber much,"

"l will fold my hands to rest for a long time."

He decided to have a little, and accumulated "littles" became the much that ruined him.

Do you indulge in excess sleep? Do you say, "This is free time, let me just enjoy much sleep?" Do you say, "The examinations are over, l can now relax, take my ease and eat the food prepared by the goddess of sleep? *" How can a soldier take time off? The apostle says, "No soldier on service gets entangled in civilian pursuits, since his aim is to satisfy the one who enlisted him"* (2 Timothy 2:4).

Those not involved in the Christian conflict can sleep and relax when they are off their regular duties, but how can a Christian, who is a soldier on active service twenty-four hours a day, take time off for that which will not contribute to the overall victory?

8. Learn to use the isolated minutes that are often wasted. The time between major activities is time which, if well used, will greatly enrich the life of a believer and increase his usefulness for the Lord. The following things can be done in the fifteen-minute periods which often fall at odd times during the day and, because these periods can come when we are at different.

Places, we suggest things that can be done anywhere

a. Pray: Fifteen minutes is good time for prayer even at a bus station or bank or office, while waiting to be served. It is better to pray silently with eyes open.

b. Witness to someone about the Lord. There are often people around.

c. Memorize a verse from the Bible. Carry Bible verses with you and memorize one during that time.

d. Read a chapter or two from the Bible. Carry a New Testament always with you.

e. Wait on the Lord. Be quiet before Him.

f. Talk to someone who may be lonely around you. Cheer him up.

g. Etc.

If you are able to handle the short periods, the longer periods will be well handled also; for he who is faithful in a little is also faithful in much.

1. Make an account of the use of your time day by day, week by week, month by month and year by year and see if you are getting closer to accomplishing your goal with passing time.

2. Repent deeply and sincerely of any waste of time and ask God to forgive you and restore you.

4.   Discipline in speech

A person of disciplined speech is truly a disciplined person. Most believers are undisciplined in their speech. The Bible says, *"The tongue of the righteous is choice silver"* (Proverbs 10:20*). "The lips of the righteous feed many"* (Proverbs 10:21). In talking about undisciplined speech, the Bible says, *"And the tongue is a fire. The tongue is an unrighteous world among our members, staining the whole body, setting on fire the cycle of nature, and set on fire by hell. For every kind of beast and bird, of reptile and sea creature, can be tamed and has been tamed by humankind, but no human being can tame the tongue - a restless evil, full of deadly poison. With it we bless the Lord and Father, and with it we curse men, who are made in the likeness of God"* (James 3:6-9).

The one who can control his tongue can control his whole body. The Bible says, *"If any one makes no mistakes in what he says, he is a perfect man, able to bridle the whole body also"* (James 3:2). The control of the tongue then will reflect something of the discipline of the whole body.

If a person is not able to say the right things, he should keep quiet. He will, by keeping silent, be mistaken for a wise man, even if he is not.

The discipline of the tongue must be goal-directed. It must help the person to accomplish his objective, which is to win

Christ and co-operate with Him in the establishment of His Kingdom in the hearts of men.

The disciplined person must ask himself before he says anything:

1. Is what l want to say true? All half-truths, exaggerations, understatements, must be eliminated from the speech of all who will go far with God. Exaggerations are lies, and the Bible says that liars are the sons of the wicked one (John 8:44) and that their lot will be in the lake that burns with fire and sulphur which is the second death (Revelation 21:8). Everything that is not wholly true must not be spoken. Anything about which there is partial doubt must not be spoken. Anything that was not heard from someone should not be said as having been heard. The believer must say that which, when said, will meet the approval of God as true. Will saying it help me to win Christ and win people for His Kingdom?

2. Is what l want to say necessary? Will it help the person to be more like Christ? Something may be true but that does not qualify it as a thing to be spoken. Each believer must ask himself, "ls it absolutely necessary to say this thing? Will saying it contribute to my winning Christ and my winning the world for Him?" If it is true but will not contribute to my winning Christ and my winning the world for Him or contribute to my winning Him for myself or benefit the person to whom l am talking, then that truth is forbidden. It must not be spoken.

3. Is the spirit in which it is being said right? Something may be true. It may, when said, help in winning Christ and in winning the world for Him, but if it is said in the wrong

spirit - partly to win Christ and partly to advertise self or to expose someone - then it should not be said at all. Anything that does not result from a very pure motive will ultimately neither fully glorify Christ nor build His Kingdom. Any right thing that is not spoken out of love for the Lord and for the world He died to save, is forbidden. It must not be spoken.

4. Is it being said to the right person? Some things may be true, necessary and could be spoken out of a pure motive for the glory of the Lord, but if spoken to the wrong person, will fail to achieve their goal and, therefore, be wrong. The Lord Jesus told the disciples, "You are clean, but not every one of you." *He said this because Judas was present and he was not clean. He talked further to them and then said, "I am not speaking of you all; I know whom I have chosen; it is that the scripture may be fulfilled, 'He who ate my bread has lifted his heel against me'"* (John 13:18). Jesus spoke about the eleven being clean, but He also ensured that He left no doubt that Judas was not included.

Another example of a different kind is to give solid spiritual food to babies. The food would then be correct but the audience not ripe for it, and that would result in a waste. It would be wasted food at best. At the worst, the babies may be led off the track completely.

5. Is it being said at the right time? Something may be right for a person but the time is wrong. He may be too young to receive it and, therefore, not able to handle it. He may have some other problem weighing on his heart and, as such, he cannot receive what is said in the right spirit. In that case, the thing intended should not be said. It is forbidden.

6. Am I the right person to say it? Something may be right, good and timely for a person to be told, but you may be the wrong person to say it to him. Take, for example, that a brother falls into sin. Who should go and talk to him and help to restore him? Certainly, it cannot just be any believer. The apostle Paul said, *"Brethren, if a bother is overtaken in any trespass, you who are spiritual should restore him in a spirit of gentleness. Look to yourself, lest you too be tempted."* (Galatians 6:1-2). It is not advisable for young believers to attempt to restore a more mature brother who has fallen into sin. Restoration is good and needed, but it is not for them to carry it out because, being young, the cross has not worked out the needed gentleness; and having not faced much temptation themselves, they lack the necessary humility that would enable them to look to themselves so that they are not tempted.

So, if you are not the right person to say it, for you, it is a forbidden affair, even though the person may need it and what is to be said to him is right and the timing right. If you sense his need, pray that the Lord should send the right person to minister to him, and the Lord is always on time!

If the thing and ourselves pass the above tests, then with humility and with boldness, let us speak out. These tests eliminate the following sins of speech:

1. Gossip
2. Harsh answers
3. Flattery
4. Lying in all forms
5. Rash speech
6. Etc.

Some words from Proverbs on speech are given below. Ponder over them.

1. *"A soft answer turns away wrath"* (Proverbs 15:1).
2. *"There is one whose rash words are like sword thrusts, but the tongue of the wise brings healing"* (Proverbs 12:18).
3. *"The mind of the righteous ponders how to answer, but the mouth of the wicked pours out evil things"* (Proverbs 15:28).
4. *"A gentle tongue is a tree of life"* (Proverbs 15:4).
5. *"He who forgives an offence seeks love, but he who repeats a matter alienates friends"* (Proverbs 17:9).
6. *"Argue your case with your neighbour himself, and do not disclose another's secret"* (Proverbs 25:9).
7. *"A word fitly spoken is like apples of gold in a setting of silver"* (Proverbs 25:11).
8. *"Like a gold ring or an ornament of gold is a wise reprover to a listening ear"* (Proverbs 25:12).
9. *"He who sings songs to a heavy heart is like one who takes off a garment on a cold day, and like vinegar on a wound"* (Proverbs 25:20).
10. *"It is a snare for a man to say rashly, 'It is holy,' and to reflect only after making his vows"* (Proverbs 20:25).
11. *"He who rebukes a man will afterward find more favour than he who flatters with his tongue"* (proverbs 28:23).
12. *"A man who flatters his neighbour spreads a net for his feet"* (Proverbs 29:5).

The last thing l want to say is that since a person often reacts to what he hears, control what you hear. Keep away from the company of people whose speech provokes you to say the wrong thing. Do not become a man who does not speak. There are many good things to talk about.

Anyone who keeps silent when he should speak is undisciplined and is equally as bad as the one who speaks when he should not speak. By keeping silent, he places his desires above those of God, quenches the Spirit and hinders God.

Talk about Jesus and His love. Witness to people. Praise and worship the Lord. Encourage and exhort. Minister life. Before you became disciplined, you used your words to minister death. Now, do the opposite. Minister life, health and healing with your words. Speech is not a terrible thing. When the tongue has been disciplined, it becomes a very useful servant that should be fully used for the glory of God. Unless it is used that way, you will not fully satisfy the call of God on your life. The answer to the abuse of speech is not "no speech" but "right speech."

You may be wondering if disciplining your speech is actually possible. You might have tried and tried but failed to go anywhere. Stop trying. Relax. Turn to the Lord and pray with the Psalmist, saying, *"Set a guard over my mouth. O Lord, keep watch over the door of my lips"* (Psalm 141:3). The Lord has heard you. He will rush to help you and, as you prepare to co-operate with the Holy Spirit, He will bring you to a mastery of your speech and, how blessed you will then be!

5.   Discipline of emotions

Emotions include among others moods, anger, sentiments, etc. Many people are governed by their emotions. But emotions can all be brought under control, so that they serve the Lord Jesus and the interests of the Kingdom. Unless this subduing of emotions takes place, things will go wrong. The Word of the Lord expects believers to bring all their emotions under control.

Take anger as an example. The Bible says, *"He who is slow to anger has great understanding, but he who has a hasty temper exalts folly"* (Proverbs 14:29). *"A hot-tempered man stirs up strife, but he who is slow to anger quiets contention"* (Proverbs 15:18). *"A fool gives full vent to his anger, but a wise man quietly holds it back"* (Proverbs 29:11).

So even if a person has cause to be angry, he can be slow about it, he can constrain himself or he can give full vent to his anger. Discipline means that a person learns and masters how to be slow to anger and refuses to give full vent to whatever may be his feelings. All who want to control their anger can.

What of moods? We know that there are:

1. High moods (state of great excitement),
2. Normal moods,
3. Low moods,
4. Depression.

The moods that a person wears are what the person decides he should wear. Even if moods come unconsciously on people, they can be put away consciously. A person who is in low moods can decide to get out of these moods and put on normal moods. This is the manifestation of discipline. The disciplined maintain normal moods almost always, and if any deviation occurs, they immediately take the situation at hand and normalize it.

Undisciplined people sway from one extreme mood to the other. They change moods as the chameleon changes colours.

In one minute they are shouting as if on top of the world and in the next minute, they are buried in deepest depression. This is what you observe on football fields. When one side scores, the supporters of the side that scored jump and rejoice exceedingly. A few minutes afterwards, the other side may score and these same people, who seemed to be on top of the world, will sink into the deepest depression.

Emotions that move from one extreme to the other at short intervals betray indiscipline. If that is your situation, you should do something about it. If you are the type of person who occasionally withdraws into himself for hours or days and sometimes weeks, do not blame it on hormones. The fault is in your will and you should do something about it. Come out of such a poor representation of Christ and do not punish the people around you with such godlessness.

What of emotions of love? Some people say, "l have fallen in love with so and so. He does not love me. l love him so much that l am hurt, but l cannot help loving him." To continue to weep over someone whom you think you love but who does not love you, is foolishness. Come out of it. It is not that person that you love. Your problem is self-love. What you are actually saying is that your emotions went away from you without control to that person and that they are continuing to feel for him in an uncontrolled manner. That being the case, the person need not take you seriously because some day, in the same uncontrolled manner, what you now feel for him could disappear or be transferred to another person.

True love comes from the heart. It responds to the laws of the heart. It flows according to the laws of the heart. By watching diligently over your heart you should be able to control what gets into it and what flows out of it. The Bible says, *"Keep your heart with all vigilance; for from it flow the springs of life"* (Proverbs 4:23). If you do not obey this injunction and are, therefore, not vigilant in watching and keeping your heart, it may flow to any direction and who is to blame? So we recommend that instead of allowing the heart to flow in some unwanted direction and then struggle to redirect it, the best thing is to discipline your heart from the beginning.

One way to do this is by disciplined surrender to the Lord. The Bible says, *"May the Lord direct your hearts to the love of God and to the steadfastness of Christ"* (2 Thessalonians 3:5). Let the Lord have all of you, and ask Him to direct your heart to the love of God. Such a heart that has been fully and completely directed to the love of God by the Lord will be prevented from loving the wrong objects and the wrong persons. I personally think that no one should love anyone or anything directly. It will always lead to confusion. I suggest that the total love of a person's heart should be poured out unto the Lord. I suggest that the command to *"Love the Lord your God with all your heart, and with all your soul, and with all your might"* (Deuteronomy 6:5) should be put into practice literally. All the total love of the believer's being should be poured out unto the Lord, and the only way that the love of such a heart can reach another person or thing is as directed to that person by the Lord. In that way, the problem of loving the wrong objects or the wrong persons is dealt with fully.

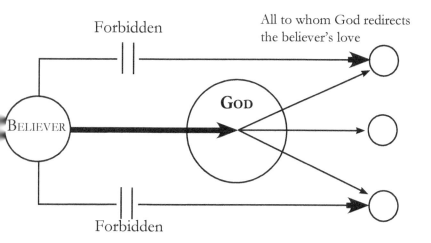

The total love of a believer's spirit, soul and body is poured out unto the Lord, and the Lord then redirects what He wants other people or things to have of the believer's love. In this way, the believer's love remains single-hearted towards the Lord and he can say with a good conscience, *"Whom have I in heaven but thee? And there is nothing upon earth that I desire besides thee"* (Psalm 73:25). Such love, controlled and directed by the Lord, will never go wrong. The question is whether believers trust the Lord enough to leave their interests in His hands. He loves them enough to take their best interest to heart. Those who trust Him completely give Him their all and know no heartaches. Those who doubt Him hold back and suffer.

The last point l want to make about this matter of discipline and emotions contains the warning given in Songs of Solomon 8:4. It says, "I adjure you, O daughters of Jerusalem, that you stir not up nor awaken love until it please." l want to suggest that you do not stir up or awaken love until it pleases the Lord to do so. Do not use words, looks, touches, etc, to awaken feelings prematurely in anyone. Do not allow anyone to use words, looks, touches to awaken feelings in you that he/she cannot satisfy or that he/she should not satisfy. So be in control of yourself and control the impact of others on you.

6.   The need for endurance

Discipline will not be achieved in the first attempt. In many areas it is a battle that goes on for long. You have to struggle against tendencies towards indiscipline. You have to resist all the tendencies towards going back to indiscipline. You are struggling against indiscipline. It is a sort of fight. Do not give up. There are times when discipline will make you momentarily unhappy. Do not bother about immediate happiness. The Bible says, "For the moment all discipline seems painful rather than pleasant." However that is not all. "Afterward it yields the peaceful fruit of righteousness to those who have been trained by it."

Discipline is training, and no training is complete overnight. If you are overweight, you will not lose all the excess weight in one day. From the beginning the change may be insignificant. Do not give up. Press on. Do not be discouraged. Lift your drooping hands and strengthen your weak knees. See that you strive to be disciplined in every area of your life. See to it that you do not fail to obtain the prize that discipline brings - a spirit, soul and body totally pliable in the hands of God the Holy Spirit.

Stop giving excuses. They will not help you. The sluggard who does not want to work says, *"There is a lion outside! I shall be slain in the streets!"* (Proverbs 22:13). If you are overweight, do not say, "l have fat bones," or "It is hereditary," or "l eat so little but grow so fat." Such excuses will help you to ease your conscience and you will remain fat. If you are undisciplined with your money so much so that you have no savings, do not excuse yourself by saying, "Well, we are told not to lay up treasures on earth." The question is, "Are you laying up treasures in heaven?" If you are late, admit it. Do not look for an excuse to justify your lateness. If you want excuses, you can produce one million of them, but you will remain undisciplined.

7.   Begin to act today

Begin to act on the contents of this message today. Act at once. Start with simple things; for the one who is disciplined in small things is also disciplined in big things.

Begin to keep all your appointments. Make sure you get to places in time. Do not be late. Allow time for the unexpected things that could come your way to prevent you from arriving there on time. Dress neatly. Pay attention to your buttons. Make sure your shoes are well polished. Make your bed neatly. Refuse to keep anything on it. When you take off a shirt from your body, hang it up or put it in the laundry basket for washing. Do not put it in one place in the hope of transferring it later on. Get your box organized. Put your wardrobe in order. Hang all clothes up in an orderly way. Brush your teeth. Refuse to break a fast before the scheduled date. You will not die from fasting for a few days or weeks. The Irish people who were on a hunger strike continued for two months before they seriously deteriorated and died. Greet people warmly. Push away all negative moods as soon as you discover that you are moody. Begin to speak all the truth. Remember that your purpose in discipline is to satisfy the Lord Jesus. Nothing can be too much to be done for Him.

Determine not to love pleasure. Love holiness. Set your eyes on the price. Buffet your body. Bring it under control. Buffet your soul and bring it under control. Discipline your spirit and bring it under control. God bless you richly along the way of discipline!

Mercy and kindness

1. MERCY

Mercy is the capacity to show love to someone who deserves hate; to pardon someone who deserves punishment; to take into confidence someone who deserves nothing but scorn. It is that attribute of God that causes Him to pardon and forgive sinners.

2. THE MERCY OF GOD

The Psalmist, in his hour of deepest need, cried out to God, *"Have mercy on me, O God, according to thy steadfast love; according to thy abundant mercy blot out my transgressions. Wash me thoroughly from my iniquity, and cleanse me from my sin"* (Psalm 51:1-2)! He was addressing the one whom he knew as the God of mercy.

God is a God of unlimited mercy. The Bible says, *"Then David said to God, 'I am in great distress; let me fall into the hand of the Lord, for his mercy is very great; but let me not fall into the hand of man'"* (1 Chronicles 21:13).

Jonah knew God as the God of unlimited mercy. When God spared repentant Nineveh, the prophet protested, saying, *"I pray thee, Lord, is not this what I said when I was yet in my country? That is why I made haste to flee to Tarshish; for I knew that thou art a gracious God and merciful, slow to anger, and abounding in steadfast love, and repentest of evil"* (Jonah 4:2).

Personally, l want to confess that l have in my life known God as the God of abounding mercy. Before l believed and after l believed l have sinned. If He had struck me dead or opened the ground so that it swallowed me up, it would have been right and fair. My being alive today and continuing in His love is only part of a testimony to His limitless mercy. When on that Day, l stand with the elect in glory, it will be obvious to me and to all who know me that l am there because of His mercy alone. l feel like singing with the hymn writer,

"Though Satan should buffet, though trials should come

Let this blest assurance control

That Christ has regarded my helpless estate

And has shed His own blood for my soul

My sin - Oh, the bliss of this glorious thought!

My sin - not in part, but the whole,

Is nailed to His cross, and l bear it no more:

Praise the Lord, praise the Lord, O my soul!"

The Lord, who is all-mercy, expects His children to be like Him in this aspect of their character.

1.   The command to be merciful

The Bible says, *"Be merciful, even as your Father is merciful"* (Luke 6:36). *"Take heed to yourselves; if your brother sins, rebuke him, and if he repents, forgive him; and if he sins against you seven times in the day, and turns to you seven times, and says, 'I repent,' you must forgive him"* (Luke 17:3-4).

The Lord Jesus told the following parable on the need for us to be merciful. He said, *"Therefore the kingdom of heaven may be compared to a king who wished to settle accounts with his servants. When he began the reckoning, one was brought to him who owed him ten thousand talents; and as he could not pay, his lord asked him to be sold, with his wife and children and all that he had, and payment to be made. So the servant fell on his knees, imploring him, 'Lord, have patience with me, and I will pay you everything.' And out of pity for him the lord of that servant forgave him the debt. But that same servant, as he went out, came upon one of his fellow servants who owed him a hundred denarii; and seizing him by the throat he said, 'Pay what you owe me.' So his fellow servant fell down and besought him, saying, 'Have patience with me, and I will pay you.' He refused and went and put him in prison till he should pay the debt. When his fellow servants saw what had taken place, they were greatly distressed, and they went and reported to their lord all that had taken place. Then his lord summoned him and said to him, 'You wicked servant. I forgave you all that debt because you besought me; and should not you have had mercy on your fellow servant, as I had mercy on you? And in anger his lord delivered him to the jailers, till he should pay all his debt. So also my heavenly Father will do to every one of you, if you do not forgive your brother from your heart"* (Matthew 18:23-35).

The Lord Jesus was here saying to all believers, "God has forgiven you your great debt owed to Him because of your sin. He paid that debt by the sacrifice of His Son on the cross. Now, you must forgive every wrong that will ever be done to you, because that is nothing in comparison to the debt l have paid for you. If, on the other hand, you are not willing to show mercy, l will let you stand on your own and let your debt be unpaid."

Dearest friend, do you hear Him? He is saying to you that if there is someone you are not willing to forgive, then you are on your own and your sin is not covered. He put it in other words, saying, *"If you forgive men their trespasses, your heavenly Father also will forgive you; but if you do not forgive men their trespasses, neither will your Father forgive your trespasses"* (Matthew 6:14). This is a most serious issue which no one should take lightly. The Lord said, *"Blessed are the merciful, for they shall obtain mercy"* (Matthew 5:7).

l do not know how it is with you. As for me, l know too well that when l stand before Him on that Day, the only condition under which l shall be accepted is that, l, as the foremost of sinners, say with the tax-collector, "God, be merciful to me a sinner!" l say this because l know that there is no day that passes without my committing enough sin in it to banish me from God's presence for ever; yet by His grace l stand. The great tragedy then is that one like me should refuse or be unwilling to forgive anyone who has wronged me in one way or the other. Would such a refusal or a reluctance not be a manifestation of extreme blindness?

Often the children of the Kingdom, like the Pharisees of old, insist upon the wrath of God on offenders or on those who have not yet seen something which, by the grace of God, they have been allowed to see. The Bible says, *"The scribes and Pharisees brought a woman who had been caught in adultery, and placing her in the midst they said to him, 'Teacher, this woman has been caught in the act of adultery. Now in the law, Moses commanded us to stone such. What do you say about her?'..... And as they continued to ask him, he stood up and said to them, 'Let him who is without sin among you be the first to throw a stone at her.' ...But when they heard it, they went away, one by one, beginning with the eldest, and Jesus was left alone with the woman standing before him. Jesus looked up and said to her, 'Woman, where are they? Has no one condemned you?' She said, 'No one, Lord.' And Jesus said; 'Neither do I condemn you; go, and do not sin again'"* (John 8:3-11). The ones who were laden with sin but not caught by man wanted immediate judgment on her. They were without mercy. The one who was without sin before God did not condemn her. What is your attitude to those who are victims of the wicked one - those who are imprisoned by sin in one way or the other? Do you, like the disciples James and John, ask the Lord, *"Lord, do you want us to bid fire come down from heaven and consume them?"* (Luke 9:54)? I am afraid that if many believers today could do it, they would have long ago called down fire to consume those who would not believe in the Lord Jesus or some believers who have failed the Lord in one way or the other. How many have wished that someone who was speaking blasphemous words against the name of the Lord was instantly struck dead or that he lost his power of speech instantly in order that his sin might be exposed? To demand God's justice is one thing, but to manifest the mercy and loving-kindness of God is another thing altogether. The Lord Jesus answered James and John with a rebuke.

How does He answer your request for immediate judgment on those who have not believed or those who have not entered into victory over sin?

2.   Growing in mercy

The apostle Paul writes, *"Forgiving each other; as the Lord has forgiven you, so you must forgive"* (Colossians 3:13). So growth in mercy will correspond to the light received from the Lord as to the depth of our personal sin and the greatness of His forgiveness. The one who sees how sinful he was and the depth from which the Lord picked him, will show more mercy to the others, and forgive more readily. The one whose eyes are yet closed to the degree of his sin, will demand more judgment on others.

While each one of us waits for more light from the Lord, we must at once begin to co-operate with God in showing mercy. We recommend the following: Make a list of all the people who have offended you in one way or the other, either by:

1. Persecuting you
2. Despising you
3. Speaking evil of you falsely
4. Frustrating your plans
5. Etc.

Do the following for each one them.

1. Ask God to cleanse your heart of any bitterness that is still lingering in it against them.
2. Forgive them in the name of Jesus.
3. Pray for them.
4. Go and visit them or write a letter to them.
5. Send them a material gift.
6. Continue to pray for them and to witness to them.

7. Love them actively.

8. Forget what they did to you that hurt you.

As you co-operate with the Holy Spirit in this way and in other ways that He will reveal to you, you will begin to make progress in the School of Mercy.

As you make progress, you will be tested. You will find out that someone you once trusted is making damaging statements about you behind your back. The immediate temptation will be to distrust that one, change your mind about him and sever all relationships with him. If you did that, you would only be doing what the world does. Because you are not of the world, show mercy to that one. Forgive him, love and trust him as before, and great will be your reward in heaven.

3. KINDNESS

If mercy, as we have just treated it, applies to people who have sinned, we see kindness as mercy to people who are in need. They do not have to be in need of pardon. They may be in need of spiritual or material things and their need is not necessarily the result of some evil that they have done.

As I think of kindness the story of the Good Samaritan in the Bible comes into my mind as a good example. It runs thus, *"A man was going down from Jerusalem to Jericho, and he fell among robbers, who stripped him and beat him, and departed, leaving him half dead. Now by chance a priest was going down that road; and when he saw him he passed on the other side. So likewise a Levite, when he came to the place and saw him, passed by on the other side. But a Samaritan, as he journeyed, came to the place where he was; and when he saw him, he had compassion, and went to him and bound up his wounds, pouring on oil and wine; then he set him on his own beast and brought him to an inn, and took care of him. And the next day he took out two denarii and gave them to the innkeeper, saying, 'Take care of him and whatever more you spend, I will repay you when I come back'"* (Luke 10:30-35).

The man who fell among thieves did not do anything to precipitate the evil that befell him. It could have been anyone going on a normal journey. He fell into the wrong hands and lost all, including his health. No one could blame him. As he lay there, he needed help very badly. No one, however, was obliged to help him. In fact, anyone who decided to help him stood the risk of getting into the same trouble into which he had gotten. The priest and the Levite passed by and went away quickly for safety to make it clear that kindness, as a fruit of the Holy Spirit, is not something that is possessed by religious men outside of vital fellowship with the Lord.

The Good Samaritan saw him and had compassion on him and went to his aid. He spent of his time, oil and wine, and walked so that this person might have a ride on the horse. He took the risk of being equally attacked, robbed, beaten and even killed by the thieves, and sacrificed his convenience and comfort for a stranger. In the inn he took care of him and when he had to leave the next day, he paid for his care and committed himself to bear any further financial expenditures on the man.

We can say that kindness is help given out of compassion to the needy who are not our legal obligation. It is motivated by compassion. The person sees the others in need and the need moves his heart to do something about it that is costly and personal.

l have seen people give away things in a very impersonal way. l do not consider this kindness. l have seen people give money to the poor, the blind, the leprous, all in a kind of condescending way that did not even give one word of love and care for the person. l have seen them throw gifts at these needy people to ease their consciences. This is not kindness. l have personally received cold, expensive gifts that have brought things but nothing of the giver, and these have not been a blessing at all.

Kindness results from the meeting of two factors: A person in need and a compassionate heart.

The need could be spiritual. The Bible says, *"For we ourselves were once foolish, disobedient, led astray, slaves to various passions and pleasures, passing our days in malice and envy, hated by men and hating one another; but when the goodness and loving kindness of God our Savior appeared, he saved us, not because of deeds done by us in righteousness, but in virtue of his own mercy"* (Titus 3:3-5).

The person could be lonely and the kindness he needs is love, care or concern. Such kindness, manifested in constant visits, loving letters, gifts of flowers, may reach out to depths that a million theoretical sermons could not reach.

These acts, nevertheless, must flow out of a heart that accepts the person and loves him as he is. l will never forget a student who was very talkative in one of the Universities l attended. He was often found with a group of noisy students and gave the impression of being surrounded by friends. One day, l visited him in his room. l was surprised when he told me that l was the first person to enter his room in three months. He was very lonely and felt totally unloved. It was near the end of term and he never returned to the University the next term. Maybe he was too lonely to come back. l felt terrible. l and all the believers in the University had let him down and failed the Lord. Had we been a bit more caring, more compassionate and kinder, we might have reached out to him, saved him from academic and personal frustration and perhaps won him for the King of glory.

How many such students are there in our Universities and colleges? How many of them live next to our houses and appartments? Do you know your neighbours and have you shown kindness to them?

It rends my heart to know that even in Local Assemblies that have known the move of God's gracious Holy Spirit, kindness in depth is often lacking. How many are lonely in our Assemblies? Where is our kindness being manifested? How many broken hearts are we mending? l was once told a story of a child of about five years of age who suddenly asked her mother, "Mummy, what does God do the whole day?" The question was embarrassing as the mother did not know the answer, so she told her to go out and play with her friends. She dutifully went out and played for a little while, but soon she was back and again asked, "Mummy, what does God spend the whole day doing?" The mother again said, "Have this cake. Go and eat it with your friends." She gladly took the cake and went outside to her friends, and this time the mother prayed that God should give her the right answer. He did, for when the daughter came back to ask her question for the third time, the answer was available and she replied, "God spends the whole day mending broken hearts and broken lives."

If God does that (and l believe that God is in this mending business today among believers as He is in the manufacturing business among unbelievers), then to fail to mend broken hearts and broken lives is to fail to imitate God.

It is too easy to give correct answers, but loving-kindness, the flow of a compassion-filled heart, will produce results that correct doctrines will not be able to produce.

Compassionate, tender-hearted people are in short supply today. We have too many whose words, even when spoken in low tones, drive a sword through a listening heart. The gifts of such people will not satisfy.

May God raise up in His Church kind people, and may their kindness include the total giving of themselves away and then their things may follow. Such a life, however, is risky. Kindness is risky business. If you follow kindness, if you are kind out of compassion and because God has worked out the tender-heartedness of His Son in you, you will often be hurt. You will be misunderstood. You will be hurt and you may be betrayed. You will bleed and you may be plundered.

Do you fear any of these things? Don't. That is what the Lord went through, and, in going through them, you will grow increasingly into His likeness, and what more can you want?

"Now to him who is able to keep you from falling and to present you without blemish before the presence of his glory with rejoicing, the only God, our Savior through Jesus Christ our Lord, be glory, majesty, dominion, and authority, before all time and now and for ever." Amen.

Praise the Lord !!!

Very important

If you have not yet received Jesus as your Lord and Saviour, I encourage you to receive Him. Here are some steps to help you,

ADMIT that you are a sinner by nature and by practice and that on your own you are without hope. Tell God you have personally sinned against Him in your thoughts, words and deeds. Confess your sins to Him, one after another in a sincere prayer. Do not leave out any sins that you can remember. Truly turn from your sinful ways and abandon them. If you stole, steal no more. If you have been committing adultery or fornication, stop it. God will not forgive you if you have no desire to stop sinning in all areas of your life, but if you are sincere, He will give you the power to stop sinning.

BELIEVE that Jesus Christ, who is God's Son, is the only Way, the only Truth and the only Life. Jesus said, «*I am the way, the truth and the life; no one comes to the Father, but by me*» (John 14:6). The Bible says, «*For there is one God, and there is one mediator between God and men, the man Christ Jesus, who gave himself as a ransom for all*» (1 Timothy 2:5-6). «*And there is salvation in no one else (apart from Jesus), for there is no other name under heaven given among men by which we must be saved*» (Acts 4:12). «*But to all who received him, who believed in his name, he gave power to become children of God...*» (John 1:12). But,

CONSIDER the cost of following Him. Jesus said that all who follow Him must deny themselves, and this includes selfish financial, social and other interests. He also wants His followers to take up their crosses and follow Him. Are you prepared to abandon your own interests daily for those of Christ? Are you prepared to be led in a new direction by Him? Are you prepared to suffer for Him and die for Him if need be? Jesus will have nothing to do with half-hearted people. His demands are total. He will only receive and forgive those who are prepared to follow Him AT ANY COST. Think about it and count the cost. If you are prepared to follow Him, come what may, then there is something to do.

INVITE Jesus to come into your heart and life. He says, *«Behold I stand at the door and knock. If anyone hears my voice and opens the door (to his heart and life), I will come in to him and eat with him, and he with me «* (Revelation 3:20). Why don't you pray a prayer like the following one or one of your own construction as the Holy Spirit leads ?

> «Lord Jesus, I am a wretched, lost sinner who has sinned in thought, word and deed. Forgive all my sins and cleanse me. Receive me, Saviour and transform me into a child of God. Come into my heart now and give me eternal life right now. I will follow you at all costs, trusting the Holy Spirit to give me all the power I need.»

When you pray this prayer sincerely, Jesus answers at once and justifies you before God and makes you His child.

Please write to me and I will pray for you and help you as you go on with Jesus Christ...

If you have received the Lord Jesus-Christ after reading this book, please write to us at the following addresse :

For Europe :

Editions du Livre Chrétien

4, Rue du Révérend Père Cloarec

92400 Courbevoie

Courriel : editionlivrechretien@gmail.com

TRUE CONVERSION
(MARK 10:17-31)

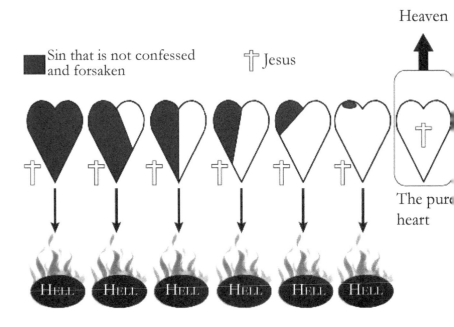

All the blemished hearts represent unsaved persons. The last pure heart alone represents the saved person.

Jesus cannot come in to blot out some of a person's sins and not others. He comes in to blot out all sins or no sin at all.

He blots out sin that is confessed and forsaken forever.

He comes in to be Saviour, Lord and King in all things and in all circumstances or He does not come in at all.

He cannot come in to be Saviour without being Lord and King because He cannot divide Himself. He is Saviour, Lord and King of all or Saviour, Lord and King of nothing at all.

Professor Zacharias Tanee Fomum

About the author

Professor Z.T. Fomum was born in 1945 in Cameroon and was taken to be with the Lord on the 14th March 2009. He was admitted to the Bachelor of Science degree, graduating as a prize-winning student from Fourah Bay College in the University of Sierra Leone. His research in Organic Chemistry earned him a Ph.D. degree in the University of Makerere, Kampala, Uganda. Recently, his published scientific work was evaluated and found to be of high distinction, earning him the award of a Doctor of Science degree from the University of Durham in Great Britain. As a Professor of Organic Chemistry in the University of Yaoundé I, Cameroon, he supervised and co-supervised more than 100 Master's and Doctoral degree theses. He published with others over 160 scientific articles in leading international journals.

The author read over 1350 books on the Christian Faith and wrote over 150 titles to advance the Gospel of Christ. 4 million copies of these books are in circulation in 11 languages, as well as 16 million gospel tracts in 17 languages. In pursuance of the purpose to proclaim the Gospel of Jesus Christ, he also made a total of over 700 missionary journeys in Cameroon and over 500 in 70 nations. These ranged from 2 days to 6 weeks in all the world's six continents.

The author led a Church-planting and missionary-sending movement, by whose ministrations, more than 10,000 healing miracles were performed by God in answer to prayer in the name of Jesus. These miracles include instant healings of; headaches, cancers, HIV/AIDS, blindness, deafness, dumbness, paralysis, madness and diverse diseases.

The author was married to Prisca Zei Fomum and they had 7 children who are all actively involved in serving the Lord. Prisca is a national and international minister specialising in the winning and discipling of children to Jesus Christ. She also communicates and imparts the vision of the ministry to children, with a view to raise and build up ministers for them.

The author owed all that he was and all that God had done in him and through him, to the unmerited favours and blessings of God and to his world wide army of friends and co-workers. He considered himself nothing without them and the blessings of God, and would have amounted to nothing but for them.

May the Lord receive all the glory!

OTHERS BOOKS BY
ZACHARIAS TANEE FOMUM

- THE CHRISTIAN WAY
- The way of life
- The way of obedience
- The way of discipleship
- The way of sanctification
- The way of Christian character
- The way of spiritual power
- The way of Christian service
- The way of spiritual warfare
- The way of overcomers
- The way of suffering for Christ
- The way of spiritual encouragement
- The way of loving the Lord
- The way of victorious praying
-

- THE PRAYER
- The ministry of fasting
- The art of intercession
- The practice of intercession
- Praying with power
- Practical spiritual warfare through prayer
- Moving God through prayer
- The ministry of praise and thanksgiving
- Waiting on the Lord in prayer
- The ministry of supplication
- Life-changing thoughts on prayer, Vol 1
- Life-changing thoughts on prayer, Vol 2
- Life-changing thoughts on prayer, Vol 3
- The centrality of prayer
-

- PRACTICAL HELPS FOR OVERCO-MERS
- The use of time
- Retreats for spiritual progress
- Personal spiritual revival
- Daily dynamic encounters with God
- The school of truth
- How to succeed in the Christian life

- The Christian and money
- Deliverance from the sin of laziness
- The art of working hard
- Knowing God – The greatest need of the hour
- Restitution : An important message for the overcomers
- Revelation a must
- True repentance
- You can receive a pure heart today
- You can lead someone to the Lord Jesus today
- The overcomer as a servant of man
- You have a talent!
- The Making of Disciples
- The secret of spiritual fruitfulness
- The dignity of manual labour
-

- GOD, SEX AND YOU
- Enjoying the premarital life
- Enjoying the choice of your marriage partner
- Enjoying the married life
- Divorce and remarriage
- A successful marriage; the husband's making
- A successful marriage; the wife's making
-

- EVANGELISATION
- God's love and forgiveness
- Come back home my son; I still love you
- Jesus loves you and wants to heal you
- Come and see; Jesus has not changed!
- 36 reasons for winning the lost to Christ
- Soul winning, Volume 1
- Soulwinning, Volume 2
- Celebrity a mask
-

- MAKING SPIRITUAL PROGRESS
- Vision, burden, action
- The ministers and the ministry of the new covenant
- The cross in the life and ministry of the believer
- Knowing the God of unparalleled goodness
- Brokenness, the secret of spiritual overflow
- The secret of spiritual rest
- Making spiritual progress, Volume 1
- Making spiritual progress, Volume 2
- Making spiritual progress, Volume 3
- Making spiritual progress, Volume 4
-
- PRACTICAL HELPS IN SANCTIFICATION
- Deliverance from sin
- Sanctified and consecrated for spiritual ministry
- The Sower, the seed and the hearts of men
- Freedom from the sin of adultery and fornication
- The sin before you may lead to immediate death: Do not commit it!
- Be filled with the Holy Spirit
- The power of the Holy Spirit in the winning of the lost
-
- OTHER BOOKS
- Are you still a disciple of the Lord Jesus?
- A broken vessel
- The joy of begging to belong to the Lord Jesus : A testimony
- Laws of spiritual success, Volume 1
- Discipleship at any cost
- The shepherd and the flock
- Spiritual aggressiveness
- The secluded worshipper
- Deliverance from demons
- Inner healing
- No failure needs to be final
- You can receive the baptism into the Holy Spirit now
- Facing life's problems victoriously
- A word to the students

- The prophecy of the overthrow of the satanic prince of Cameroon
- The power to operate miracles
-
- NEW BOOKS
- Church Planting Strategies
- Delivrance from the Sin Of The Gluttony
- God Centredness
- God, Money And You
- In The Crucible For Service
- Issues Of The Heart
- Jesus Saves And Heals Today
- Leading A Local Church
- Meet The Liberator
- Power For Service
- Prayer And A Walk With God
- Prayer crusade Volume 1
- Revolutionary Thoughts On Spiritual Leadership
- Roots And Destinies
- Spiritual Fragrance
- Spiritual Gifts
- Spiritual Nobility
- The Art Of Worship
- The Believer's Conscience
- The Character And Personality Of The Leader
- The Leader & His God
- The Overthrow Of Principalities And Powers
- The Processes Of Faith
- The Spirit Filled Life
- Victorious Dispositions
- Walking With God
- Women Of The Glory Vol 1
- Women Of The Glory Vol 2
- Women Of The Glory Vol 3
- You, Your Team And Your Ministry

Imprimé en France par CPI
en septembre 2019

Dépôt légal : septembre 2019
N° d'impression : 154151